Ed Robbin

Woody Guthrie and Me

Woody Guthrie and Me

AN INTIMATE REMINISCENCE

by

Edward Robbin

LANCASTER-MILLER PUBLISHERS
BERKELEY, CALIFORNIA, 1979

Contents

Acknowledgements

The lyrics in this volume have been used by permission, as follows:

Better World
  Words & Music by Woody Guthrie
  TRO—©1963 & 1976 Luclow Music, Inc., New York, N.Y.

This Land Is Your Land
  Words & Music by Woody Guthrie
  TRO—©1956, 1958 & 1970 Ludlow Music, Inc., New York, N.Y.

Pastures of Plenty
  Words & Music by Woody Guthrie
  TRO—©1960 & 1963 Ludlow Music, Inc., New York, N.Y.

So Long It's Been Good To Know Yuh
  (Dusty Old Dust)
  Words & Music by Woody Guthrie
  TRO—©1940 (renewed 1968), 1950 (renewed 1978) and 1951 (renewed 1979) Folkways Music Publishers, Inc., New York, N.Y.

Do Re Mi
  Words & Music by Woody Guthrie
  TRO—©1961 & 1963 Ludlow Music, Inc., New York, N.Y.

Vigilante Man
  Words & Music by Woody Guthrie
  TRO—©1961 & 1963 Ludlow Music, Inc., New York, N.Y.

Don't You Push Me Down
  Words & Music by Woody Guthrie
  TRO—©1954 Folkways Music Publishers, Inc., New York, N.Y.

Jesus Christ
  Words & Music by Woody Guthrie
  TRO—©1961 & 1963 Ludlow Music, Inc., New York, N.Y.

Here's Pete with a paint bucket on his arm, climbing the mast of the Good Ship Clearwater, which has done so much to clean up the Hudson River. Photo by John Putnam. ▲

Foreword

AS THE DECADES ROLL ON, more and more people recognize the influence Woody Guthrie has had, not only on our music but also on the political and social life of our nation.

Why?

He wrote songs that echoed in the hearts of millions of men and women and children and helped them give voice to their own needs and desires.

Most of these songs have never had any great commercial success on the air waves. But they have gone from person to person until we all know them:

> *This land is your land*
> *This land is my land*
> *From California to the New York Island.*
> *From the redwood forest*
> *To the gulf stream waters*
> *This land was made for you and me.*©

He wrote narrative ballads as well, and songs for children and hymns to the spirit of resistance and people's unity. The songs have the genius of simplicity, and they flow from a strong tradition. Woody's faith in the masses of working people and his stubborn insistence on following a noncommercial path remind us of other national bards, such as Taras Shevchenko of the Ukraine, Robert Burns of Scotland, and Atahualpa Yupanqui of Argentina.

Like them, he developed as an atrist and as a political thinker because the social upheavals of his youth brought him in contact with people he might not otherwise have met. Woody showed tens of thousands of others how they, too, could write songs, borrowing from tradition and adding to it from their own lives and thoughts.

This book, by detailing how Woody continued his education after he left Oklahoma for California, can serve as a source book for any future analysis of his life and songs. We are fortunate that Ed Robbin has taken the time to set down these details, which he knew first hand. He was the working journalist, just a couple years older than Woody, who introduced Woody to a working people's movement that, in turn, took Woody to its heart.

Woody said to them, and to us, and to future generations, *don't give up, don't ever give up.*

> *There's a better world a-coming, wait and see, see, see.*
> *There's a better world a-coming, wait and see.*
> *Out of rumbling and of rattling*
> *Out of armies battling*
> *There's a better world a-coming, wait and see.*©

Pete Seeger
Beacon, New York

The author, Ed Robbin (on the right) in 1975, on the set of *Bound for Glory* at Isleton, California with (left to right) Joady Guthrie (who worked as an extra on the film), Clara Robbin, and Mary Guthrie. Photo © Copyright 1975, by United Artists. ▲

A Word
from the Author

THESE PAGES are the story of how I met Woody Guthrie, how we became friends and neighbors. They also describe the events, social and political, from which Woody emerged. There never was a poet or writer who more clearly expressed the feelings, the passions, the humor, the very voice of his people.

Though some things I tell took place more than forty years ago, they are deeply engraved in my memory. Through the years, like the troubadours who traveled to sing the happenings of their day, I have been called on to tell my tale about Woody and his times over and over. Nevertheless, I must remind the reader that except for my long talk with Will Geer, which I taped, the words I cite in quotation marks are from my recollection. They ring in my head as though spoken yesterday, but do not hang me from a tree if they are not exactly as spoken.

Edward Robbin
Berkeley, California

Nostalgia

WOODY WILL NOT LET ME ALONE. Woody Guthrie, the man who wrote more than a thousand songs, the man whose songs, anecdotes, and writings are now entwined in the folk heritage of this country, was a friend and a colleague of mine in his beginnings. That's what this book is about—my memories of that period.

This wiry little fellow with a tousled head of hair, worn boots, denim work pants, an old guitar, his head up and something of a swagger in his walk—I knew him soon after he came to Los Angeles in the late thirties, still covered with the dust of his migration from Oklahoma and Texas, this hobo of the freight trains, field worker, singer, teller of tales, this child of the Depression and the war years.

Why has he become a part of the saga of this land, a legend among the guitar-toting youths of the world?

Dead for more than a dozen years and hospitalized almost fifteen years before he died, his name lives and grows with the passing of time. He lived next door to me, pounded on his type-writer through half the night, played his guitar, and sang songs for my kids and his in our backyard.

Woody will not let me alone.

Through the years a stream of people have come to see me, people who were collecting information for books, for doctoral theses, or for performances of various kinds. Many of them asked me to put down my recollections of the period when Woody and I were close.

Then several years ago I was in Paris and visited with Tom Van Dycke. Tom worked on the *People's World* as sports editor while I was on the staff, at the time I met Woody. When I visited him in Europe, Tom had been living in a village just outside of Paris for twenty years or so. He was a foreign correspondent during World War II. In 1948 he covered the war in Palestine and the creation of the new state of Israel. For years he was associated with the great French playwright, Marcel Pagnol, who did the *Fanny* series and *The Baker's Wife*. Despite this colorful and eventful life, Tom's nostalgia is still for the period of the thirties in Los Angeles.

Tom is a hunched, big-chested man with a long face and a pointed gray beard. After all these years in Paris he is like a Frenchman, with his flailing arms and his speech, whether in English or French, tumbling out of his mouth like a waterfall.

He took me to a favorite restaurant in a little alley not far from the American Express. Claude, the proprietor, greeted Tom warmly. Tom paid up an old debt from a bet they had made on the elections. Claude brought a very special bottle of wine. Tom sniffed the bouquet and sent it back.

"Come on, Claude, you can do better than that. Give me wine, not swill." He named a wine and a year he wanted.

For years Tom had been urging me to write about the thirties and particularly about Woody.

"How you met him and nurtured him. That's the story no one except you can tell. You recognized his importance when other people, including me, saw him as just another hillbilly. Maybe you don't know that even in Europe Woody is big."

It was late afternoon when we left the restaurant and took a cab to Montmarte. He told the driver to take us to the foot of Montmarte where a wide set of concrete steps leads to the square.

We climbed the steps. Midway I turned to look at the city — the lumbering of traffic and the shrill sounds of the bleating horns had dropped to a murmer; scattered church spires and jumbled rooftops, like children's blocks, lay below us. The setting sun flashed light and golden from the windows of the taller buildings.

Young people — Americans, Germans, and some Scandinavians — were gathered in a plaza on top of Montmarte.

They wore denims and boots. Some were draped in colorful pieces of costumes they had picked up in travels through Turkey or the Mideast. Many toted guitars and some had harmonicas, banjos, or mandolins. They sat or lay around on the steps, idly picking on their instruments or talking and resting.

Tom got into conversation with a German youth, who said he had come from Munich and was on his way to Turkey. They spoke German, in which Tom was fairly fluent.

"Have you ever heard of Woody Guthrie?" Tom asked.

"Woody?" the boy laughed. "O.K." He picked up his guitar, tossed back his long blond hair, and started to sing. "So long, it's been good to know ya." He sang it in English, then in German.

"How come you know about Guthrie?" Tom asked.

"We all know about him." He waved. "He is for us very important."

"But why?" Tom persisted. "He's been dead a long time and his songs were only about American things."

Then, still strumming on the guitar, the boy murmured in German, "Wunderbar, der Woody. Er spricht zu mir."

As we walked away, Tom said, "You see what I mean, Ed? Woody's songs and his spirit are alive here. I guess, wherever there are young people. Go back and write your part of his story."

*I*t's a mighty hard road that my poor hands have hoed,
My poor feet have traveled this hot, dusty road,
On the edge of your cities you'll see me and then
I come with the dust and I'm gone with the wind.©

Woody Guthrie Folk Songs, p. 22

Salinas: Fascism in America

I CAME TO CALIFORNIA in the early thirties, after spending four years in Palestine. There I had worked on an English newspaper in Jerusalem and lived the communal life on a kibbutz. Perhaps that kibbutz life prepared me for the kind of political life I would enter in California. For in Los Angeles I soon found myself in a welter of social and political upheaval.

We were in the heart of the Depression. Most people who read or think about the thirties see in their mind's eye the apple vendors and the long lines at soup kitchens. I saw and tasted those, and unemployment and the WPA, too.

But these are not the important things about the thirties. Most significant is what followed as a result of those hardships. The American people were awakened, roused to anger and organization. The unemployed organized and marched to Washington, demanding jobs and relief. Under John L. Lewis, the millions of industrial workers throughout the land organized into industrial unions. There was a wave of sit-down strikes in Detroit and other eastern cities. And in our own City of the Angels and environs, the fledgling aircraft industries were struck by young workers who sat and would not budge until their unions were recognized. The open-shop county of Los Angeles was shaken to its roots, by the militant strikes of those years and by the political and social turmoil of the times.

The struggle against fascism and Naziism, and later the attempt to gain support for the Loyalist government of Spain and the fight for collective security in the League of Nations — all these were part of the thirties. So, too, was the recall election in Los Angeles. That election overturned the corrupt and reactionary city administration. And statewide that election accomplished the almost revolutionary defeat of the entrenched state government and the election of Culbert Olson as governor of the state. More of all that later.

It was in that milieu that I became interested in the migrant workers, about three years before I met Woody. Many people are curious about how so many folks turned to radicalism in the thirties. And I was impressed, even then, when I occasionally met friends I had known in other parts of the country, to find that they, too, had moved into political activity. Some had become Communist party members, others were Trotskyites. This became a cause in the early thirties, when we could still tolerate opposition, of long arguments deep into the night. Most of us got our formal socialist education from the writings for the English interpreter of Marxism, John Strachey. But principally we learned from the convulsion in our society.

It was nearly 1936. Los Angeles newspaper headlines were blazing with stories about atrocities the strikers were supposedly committing in the Salinas valley. The public was aroused. Would they have salad if there was no lettuce crop?

The country and the state of California were in ferment. Everywhere industrial workers were organizing. Franklin Roosevelt was running for a second term. The Soviet Union was pleading at the League of Nations for a collective agreement among the Western nations to stop Hitler and the spread of fascism. Litvinoff was eloquent but he spoke to deaf ears. The civil war was raging in Spain, and it affected us as if it were in our own backyard.

One evening as I was walking aimlessly on Spring Street in Los Angeles I noticed a hand-printed sign calling for a meeting of citizens to discuss the Salinas lettuce strike. The meeting was to be at the office of the International Labor Defense at 8 P.M.

It was close to eight, and out of idle curiosity I drifted into the scroungy building, took an antiquated elevator up a few flights, and walked into a desolate meeting hall. The walls were

covered with old posters calling for the defense of Tom Mooney and Warren Billings and other political prisoners. There were pictures of the Scottsboro boys on the walls, appeals for funds, posters with the faces of Georgi Dimitroff, the Bulgarian anti-

Nazi, and Leo Gallagher, a radical labor attorney. Six or eight other people were scattered around on the yellow folding chairs.

After twenty minutes, when sixteen or eighteen people had gathered, an elderly man with a wizened face and bright blue eyes beat a gavel on the worn table and called the meeting to order. The chairman announced that this was a meeting of the citizens of Los Angeles and that we had gathered to discuss the strike of the lettuce workers. Organization of migrant farm workers was long past due. Ways must be found to support their fledgling organization, which had shown the courage to take on the growers in Salinas.

There were a few farm workers in the audience, and some of the radicals who attended such meetings and were always on hand to distribute leaflets or raise money for good causes. Several took the floor to say that the workers' side of the story was not being told in the press. I stood up and said that there should be a way to find out what was happening and get the real story to the public.

Immediately someone suggested that there ought to be a citizens' committee chosen to investigate the strike and report back its findings. Before I knew what was happening, I had been selected, along with two kindly looking old ladies, to go to Salinas and get the facts. One of the women was the wife of a well-known owner of a rare-book shop in downtown Los Angeles; the other was the head librarian of one of the public libraries. The two women were friends and had worked together for other causes.

The next day we drove to Salinas in my vintage Chevrolet. As we approached the town we were halted by highway patrolmen, who had barricaded the road and were stopping all cars. I explained that we were a citizens' committee who had come to investigate the strike and that we wanted to speak to representatives of the growers and the strike leaders. Apparently we looked respectable and harmless. So they let us through and directed us to the headquarters of the growers, at the main hotel in town.

In spite of the air of terror and violence in the city of Salinas, our committee moved freely through the town—I suppose, because of these two very respectable women. We went to the Jeffery Hotel where the growers, the vigilantes, and the top city officials had set up their headquarters, and we interviewed whatever leaders we could buttonhole about the causes of the strike and the violence.

Then we went to the workers' strike headquarters, which had been set up in the flat of one of the strike leaders. The workers showed us the bullet holes in the walls, the broken glass, and some of the children still sick with doses of tear gas. When we told these strikers that we were sent by the International Labor Defense, we got a warm welcome and everyone wanted to tell us their stories.

We rode out to the picket lines and joined the march with the strikers. Whole families of strikers were on the line, including women and children. Deputy sheriffs, highway police, and goons were on the sidelines, many carrying rifles and clubs, shouting taunts and insults.

We returned to Los Angeles that night, shaken and sobered by what we had seen. For after talking it over, the three of us agreed that we had witnessed not just a strike situation, but an example of fascist rule in the town of Salinas. A city surrounded by police, city officials, growers, and scab herders with their headquarters in the Jeffery Hotel, violence in the streets and on the picket lines: weren't these the very ingredients of Nazi and fascist rule we had been studying in the European scene?

This, then, was what I reported to a meeting of the International Labor Defense and then in a series of articles in the *Progressive News*, a small local weekly mainly engaged in exposing corruption in state and civic affairs. Soon I was asked to speak on Salinas at various meetings of unions and organizations. Then I wrote an article, for *The Nation*, which appeared in October of 1936 under the title "The General Takes Charge." I said in part: "What may be found today in Salinas, California, is perhaps the first open alliance in America of industry and government to crush civil rights. This is the definition of fascism."

I was no longer a "parlor pink," talking politics and social action without doing anything. Salinas had ended that. After the appearance of my story in *The Nation*, I was asked to speak at the forthcoming Writers Congress in San Francisco, the first of its kind in the West.

At that congress there was a new atmosphere and purpose—writers getting together to see how they could contribute to the emergent working class organization and to the anti-fascist struggle.

After I had told these writers my Salinas story, I asked how it was possible for a city to institute a reign of terror and, except for a few scattered articles in the liberal and radical papers, not a word to be heard above the din of the capitalist press. Where were the writers who should have flooded the country with pamphlets, imaginative leaflets, and books stirring people to action against the growth and spread of the Nazi fungus?

Describing the congress in a burst of youthful eloquence, I wrote:

> Down from the ivory tower and up from the garret, from penthouse studios and hall bedrooms, the shaggy, the lean, the bald, the tousled, the fat, the bitter, jaundiced screen writer, pamphleteer, novelist, poet and pulp writer, people of the typewriter and the pen gathered in San Francisco for three November days to discuss the common problems of their craft in a changing world. We who have valued above all else isolation and seclusion, who have met in the past only to bicker over schools of writing, have unprecedently begun to converge in a vast movement of congresses in Paris, London, Chicago, and now San Francisco. To discuss how to sell what we write, how to write the things that need to be said in such a way as to reach the great masses of the people, how to fight reaction and ignorance, how to secure for our craft decent working conditions, how to fight the invasion of fascism.

Having been spurred into activity by the Salinas strike, shortly afterward I went out to Douglas Aircraft in Santa Monica, where a sit-down strike was going on. I barged into strike headquarters and offered to help with the publicity. This strike was similar to the sit-downs in Detroit and other places where the newly organized Committee for Industrial Organization, or CIO, was making its bid for power. The story of the Douglas strike reflects what was happening—the new awareness and militance that were developing among industrial workers.

Learning from the sit-down strikes of the automobile workers in Detroit, aircraft workers at the Douglas plant laid down their tools and refused to leave the plant. That was in February of 1937. When I got to the plant, only 341 workers had closed the plant by sitting down and refusing to budge. These youngsters were at the windows waving to the thousands of Douglas workers and their families who stood on the other side of the street, with a cordon of police in between.

Santa Monica then was a relatively small community where people knew each other. No doubt many of the workers had brothers and cousins among the police and there was good-natured bantering back and forth. These young aircraft workers, many of them just out of high school, were shocked to find the newspapers, even their own local paper, printing a distorted version of their grievances and strike action.

On the 22nd of February, the court issued felony indictments against 341 sit-down strikers. Thousands of their fellow workers massed in the rain opposite the plant, cheering them and booing the police who led them to jail. When Donald Douglas urged the police to use tear gas to get the workers out of the plant, he was told that the chemicals could set off fires that would burn the boys alive. Douglas was quoted as replying, "Let them burn and be damned."

The 341 workers were quckly released from jail, and the newspapers announced that the strike was broken. But the next day there were fifteen hundred workers on the picket line and only a fraction of the total work force returned to work. In the end Douglas was compelled to recognize the union and negotiate a contract.

In those days political lessons were learned rapidly. I remember watching a newsboy hawking the *Los Angeles Times* on the picket line. Not one copy of the paper was sold.

After these and similar experiences, I decided to join the Communist party. I went to work for the *Western Worker*, the party organ, and in 1938 became a staff member of the newborn daily *People's World*.

I see a better world a-comin', yes, I know and I know
I see a better world a-comin, yes, I know.
Out of our storms and winds and rains,
Out of sorrow, out of pain,
I see a better world a-comin', that I know.©

Woody Guthrie Folk Songs, p. 193

How I Came
to Know
Woody Guthrie

IN 1938 I WAS LOS ANGELES editor for the *People's World*, then a daily newspaper published in San Francisco. Toward the end of the year, I managed to start a radio program of daily news commentary slanted to the left, in which I talked about the struggles of workers and unions, and against war and fascism. Woody Guthrie with his "gittar" was on the air just before me. The owner of the station, J. Frank Burke, was a squat, white-haired old man who was deeply involved in the liberal politics of Los Angeles. Burke permitted me air time when other stations would not sell time to radicals, and he had taken Woody on on what was called a sustaining program. Woody was not paid for his performance, nor did he buy his time. But he sold mimeographed copies of his songs to his listeners for a quarter.

Woody and I had a passing acquaintance. I waved to him as he came in, and we said hello as I rushed out to cover the news, write a daily column, prepare my next day's script, and do the things that people do on small, understaffed publications.

One day Woody stopped me and said, "Why don't we go out and have a beer together after your program?" He continued, "I usually stay around and listen to you, anyway, and there are a few things I'd like to just kind of talk over with you, if you don't mind."

So I said, "Sure, Woody, let's do that." And after my program, which he had been watching and listening to just outside the glass, we went down to a local bar and sat in the corner.

I asked Woody how he happened to be singing there at KFVD, and then a dialog developed which I present here as I have reconstructed it from memory.

"Well, it all happened kind of accidental—fact is, I earn a dollar bill wherever I can, and, though they don't pay me any-

Woody (far left), with a group he played with at cabarets and bars in Texas, before he came to California. Courtesy Woody Guthrie Publications, Inc.▼

thing at KFVD, I get a few little contributions from the audience. What happened was, I heard that KFVD was a place where a fella had a chance, so I went up there one day with my guitar, and knocked on Frank Burke's door. I sat down with Mr. Burke and I said, 'Mr. Burke, I'd like to sing on this here station of yours, if you'd let me, and I don't need any money for it, I just want to sing my songs.'"

Burke asked what kind of songs Woody wanted to sing and said that the station already had Stuart Hamblin, a pretty well-known western cowboy singer.

But Woody told Mr. Burke that his songs were different from Stuart Hamblin's. "His songs are pretty and nice, I guess. Mine aren't so pretty, but they're songs that I learned or I wrote while I was doing stoop labor up and down the highways and byways of California, travelin' with my people in their broken-down old cars and with their kids with bellies swollen from hunger, their mouths full of the dust of Oklahoma. They were fighting to live somehow or other, in the shanties, and with the whole family workin' out there in the fields. That is the kind of song that I'm singin', and believe me, there's thousands of my people out there who would eventually be listenin' because they want someone to speak out for 'em. Why don't you try me for a while and see what kind of response we get?"

Mr. Burke finally gave Woody a go and let him have a half hour every day. "We'll see what kind of letters you draw."

"And," Woody continued, "that's the way it all started. But now I'll ask you a question. I always listen to your program, Ed. How come you never listen to mine?"

I didn't say that I had just assumed that he was singing run-of-the-mill western songs, full of "run little doggies" and "hosses" in the sunset.

I said, "Woody, that's true. Tomorrow I will for sure."

"The other thing, Ed, is I heard you telling about this Tom Mooney. But I never heard of him and I didn't quite get the story."

"Well, Woody, this story goes all the way back to 1916 in San Francisco. That was a presidential campaign year and the big issue was preparedness. How old were you then, Woody?"

"Must have been about four. I was born on July 14, 1912."

"Bastille Day. You were really foreordained to be a revolutionary. And me — I was born on July 4th. That makes us quite a pair. And how come they named you Woodrow Wilson?"

"Guess my daddy was just a real good Democrat and I know he greatly admired Wilson. Figured Wilson would keep us out of the war."

"Anyway," I continued, "all through the country they were holding preparedness parades and on the other hand the radicals were on the soap boxes talking against militarism and imperialism and I guess Wilson was busy assuring people if he was reelected he wouldn't let us be dragged into that European war that had been going on for two years.

"Well, a parade was organized in San Francisco. It was a real military demonstration and thousands marched right down Market Street. It was also meant to be an anti-labor demonstration, to warn the rising labor movement in San Francisco that employers wouldn't stand for any nonsense from the unions. There was a wave of reaction and strikebreaking across the country coupled with jingoism."

"Where did Mooney fit into the picture?" Woody asked.

"Tom Mooney at that time was the most important labor leader in San Francisco. He had just been defeated in an attempt to organize the United Railroads Carmen. On the 22nd of July, between noon and two o'clock, this great parade of people in their uniforms, military and fraternal costumes, with flags waving and bands playing, started their march from the Embarcadero, off lower Market Street. Thousands of people who loved a parade lined the streets to cheer and wave their little flags and pennants.

"Just before two o'clock, as the parade reached Stuart and Market, a dynamite bomb exploded right by a saloon wall. It killed six people and injured about forty. The reason I have all this in mind, Woody, is that I've been reading up on it because I'm having Tom Mooney on my program in a few days. He has just been released from jail after having spent twenty-two years in the pen."

"Twenty-two years — I've been locked up two or three days and I wrote many a prison song about how vile it was — but twenty-two years — that's hard to imagine. What happened after the explosion?"

"Five days later Mooney and a twenty-two-year-old friend

and helper, Warren Billings, and a number of other union people were rounded up and arrested. There was an atmosphere of hysteria and antiunion frenzy whipped up by the press. Mooney and Billings were quickly tried and sent to San Quentin. Mooney was sentenced to hang and Billings to a life sentence."

"Did they do it or were they framed?"

"After they went to jail, defense committees were organized and the long processes of appeals were put in motion. Through the years more and more evidence was accumulated showing that both men were innocent. The principal witness was shown to be a perjurer, and the whole thing was a frame-up by police and prosecutor intended to break the growing power of labor. In 1918 President Wilson brought pressure on the governor to commute the hanging sentence to life imprisonment.

"In later years the prosecution was shown to have manufactured evidence and bribed witnesses. The jurors who were still alive appealed for clemency. But the case became a political football and they were never able to get a new trial."

Not long after Woody and I had this talk, I interviewed Mooney on my program. How strange it was to talk to this man who had just spent twenty-two years in jail. He was a short, solidly built man with iron gray hair, balding, as I remember. All through the years from his jail cell he had commanded the efforts for his defense, helped build the nationwide defense committee, sent out communiques, and never faltered in his belief that in the end he would be vindicated and released.

It was difficult to interview Mooney. In response to each question he would launch into fulminating oratory. Tom Mooney had become, for him, a cause that existed apart from himself. When I tried to ask him how he had survived all those years in prison and what life was like during those hours, days, and years, he looked puzzled and then went off again into speeches about the committee, the work, and the victory.

The day after the interview with Mooney, I kept my word to Woody and stayed to listen to his program.

"I got a little song I want to sing for my friend Ed and for all the folks out there. It's about this fella Tom Mooney, who's just got out of jail after spending twenty years for something he never done." He sang a ballad of Tom Mooney, telling the whole Mooney story and the tale of the long struggle for his release. Then he sang some of his dust bowl ballads with easy, rambling, homey talk between songs.

Woody received more mail than anyone else at the station. Many of the letters contained quarters and dollars and pencil-scrawled messages. The people who listened to him were the people he sang about, his own people, the Okies. Those were the days of Steinbeck's *Grapes of Wrath* and Carey McWilliams' *Factories in the Field*. Thousands of refugees from the dust bowl were trying to find homes and food for their children.

Later Woody was to see the picture *Grapes of Wrath* and write, "The *Grapes of Wrath* is about us pullin' out of Oklahoma and Arkansas and down south and driftin' around over the state of California, busted, disgusted, down and out and lookin' for work. Shows you how come us got to be that way. Shows the damn bankers, men that broke us and the dust that choked us, and it comes right out in plain English and says what to do about it."

Now Woody sang:

> *So long, it's been good to know ya,*
> *This dusty old dust is getting my home,*
> *And I got to be drifting along.*
> *A dust storm hit and it hit like thunder;*
> *It dusted us over, it dusted us under;*
> *It blocked out the sun,*
> *And straight for home the people did run.*©

After the program I asked Woody who wrote all those songs.

"Some of them I wrote, and some I picked up here and there and changed or just rewrote, and some are old folk songs."

"Well, how many of these songs do you have, Woody?" I asked.

"I got a whole barrel of them. I lost one big book of songs while I was wandering around the state, but I've got a couple of books here with me that I usually carry along."

"Woody, how would you like to come out to my house tonight and have dinner with us and give me a chance to look through your songs?"

"Fine with me."

And so he hopped into my old Chevy and we drove over to my house. At that time I was living in Echo Park, at 1961 Preston. This was a house that I had bought, the first house that I ever owned. It was really a small cottage, sitting on a hill. It had a living room, a tiny bedroom, a kitchen, and a big backyard. The inside walls were all knotty pine. The house, though small, was cozy and warm.

After dinner, I picked up the folders that Woody had brought along and read through the songs. I was deeply impressed with the wonderful lyric descriptions of all his experiences as a migratory worker and his songs about the dust storms that he had experienced in Oklahoma and Texas, and by the many outlaw songs that he had already written at that time.

This was the night that the great rally, sponsored by the Communist party, to celebrate the freedom of Tom Mooney, was to be held at the Trinity Auditorium. So I said to Woody, "You know, Woody, there is this big rally for Tom Mooney tonight in downtown Los Angeles, and I'd very much like you to come there and sing this ballad to Tom Mooney, if you're willing to do it."

And he said, "Sure, why not?"

"Well, I would like you to know, Woody, that this is sponsored by the Communist party, and it's a politically left-wing gathering."

And Woody said, "Left wing, right wing, chicken wing—it's the same thing to me. I sing my songs wherever I can sing 'em. So if you'll have me, I'll be glad to go."

So we got the family together—my wife Clara, Dan, about ten, and Tamara, our four-year-old—and we all trundled over to the auditorium.

At that time, it was not the usual thing at a political rally to have entertainers, and interest in folk music had hardly begun. So it was somewhat difficult to persuade the people who were running this rally to let this western hillbilly singer get on the platform and sing songs. I had to do a lot of pleading and persuading to get them to agree to let Woody sing.

The Trinity Auditorium was jammed that night. The main speakers were Robert Minor, a national Communist leader, and, of course, Tom Mooney. In addition, it was customary to have, not one or two, or even four or five, but many other speakers. They'd have a speaker for youth, and a speaker for women's rights, and then a speaker who represented a certain section of labor, and so on.

About ten o'clock that night they got around to letting Tom Mooney speak to the audience. Tom Mooney went on and on. Then there was a question-and-answer period after that. It must have been eleven o'clock before there was any hint that Woody would be allowed to play his guitar and sing his songs.

By this time part of the audience, at least, had left the auditorium. Woody, sitting on the stage, was fast asleep. However, when Mooney finally finished speaking, I nudged Woody and he got up before the microphone. He wandered a bit with anecdotes about how we had met at the station, and how he had just written a ballad that he'd like to sing to the audience. And then he sang his Tom Mooney ballad. Well, the house came down. Then Woody sang his dust bowl ballads.

Mind you, this was shortly after Culbert Olson had become governor of California in one of the great political upsets of this state. Olson had been chief lieutenant for Upton Sinclair in Sinclair's bid for the governorship in 1934. In 1939, Olson overturned the long reign of an entrenched reactionary Republican administration. One of the factors in this political revolution had been the plight of thousands of migrant farm workers who had poured into California in spite of vigilantes and state police. The migrant workers were oppressed, beaten, and exploited. They lived in shacks, dumps, under bridges, their kids running dirty and half-naked in the fields. They picked the fruits and followed the crops. And they kept pouring into the state, fleeing from the black dust and the bankruptcy of their lives in Texas and Oklahoma.

And here was this skinny guy on the stage, the very embodiment of these young people, speaking their language in bitter humor and song, with the dust of his traveling still on him, a troubadour, a balladeer, a poet, drawling:

Oh, if you ain't got the do re mi, boys,
If you ain't got the do re mi,
Better go back to beautiful Texas,
Oklahoma, Kansas, Georgia, Tennessee.
California's a garden of Eden, a paradise
To live in or see,
But believe it or not, you won't find
It so hot,
If you ain't got the do re mi.©

And that's how Woody really felt. He always said, "Kids first. Hoboes second. Rich folks last."* He said it in the songs he sang.

This song had a more direct, pertinent meaning than we get out of it today. Woody and his people had been stopped at state borders and harrassed by the state police, as though they were from a foreign country. He wrote a song about the harrassment, too.

Oh, why does a vigilante man,
Why does a vigilange man carry that sawed-off shotgun
In his hand?
Would he shoot his brother and sister down?

Have you seen that vigilante man?
Have you seen that vigilante man?
Have you seen that vigilante man?
I been hearing his name all over this land.©

After the Mooney meeting, Woody came home with us. He wrapped himself in a blanket and went to sleep on the floor. He stayed over because I had promised to drive him home in the morning. I figured it would be a good chance for us to get to know each other.

When Clara and I awoke in the late morning, Woody was already out in the back yard with our two small kids, Tamara

Woody Sez, p. 37.

and Danny, playing some songs for them, examining Danny's
chickens. They were all good friends.

After breakfast, Woody and I set out for Glendale. That was
the first I knew that Woody had a family, a wife and two children. We drove to the outskirts of Glendale, where we found
Mary and two little girls in a broken down, one-room shack.

"Where ya been?" asked Mary. "I ain't seen you for three
days."

The kids hugged Woody's leg and he patted them on the
head. Then he introduced me to Mary and told her he'd been
singing at a big meeting.

In the months after that meeting I saw a great deal of
Woody. We met at the station daily, and he frequently came to
the house. There, he would sit in the backyard picking out tunes
or talking and playing with our children. I would hear him
through the window, picking out new songs. I was astonished.
Never had I heard any adult sing from a child's point of view.
These were a new and different kind of children's songs. Actually, Woody had come up with a children's folk music that
expressed in song the thoughts, dreams, and games of the young
ones:

> *Why, oh why, or why,*
> *Because, because, because.*©

> *Don't you push me, push me, push me,*
> *Don't you push me down.*©

I became an informal booking agent for him. In those days
there were so many causes that each night he was asked to sing
at some fund-raising party in the homes or union halls. He
would get five or ten dollars for each gig, if he remembered to
appear. Of course, he had his own ideas about what fees should
really be. He said, "If you are afraid I wouldn't go over in your
lodge or party, you are possibly right. In such case, just mail me
$15 and I won't come. When I perform, I cut it down to $10. When
for a good cause, $5. When for a better cause, I come free. If you

can think of a still better one, I'll give you my service, my guitar, my hat, and sixty-five cents cash money."*

After some months Woody came to my office at the *People's World* and said, "Ed, I'd like to do a column for the paper—just little comments on things the way I see them. What do you think?"

I said, "I'd like to see some and then I'll see what I can do."

So he pulled a bunch of papers out of his pocket. There must have been twenty or thirty sheets, each with a short piece, each one illustrated, because Woody was also an excellent artist and cartoonist. I read them with delight and sent the batch to Al Richmond, editor of the *People's World*.

Al was making an effort to reach out to a larger audience by having more popular features in the paper. For example, the backpage was made up of sports columns, particularly good pieces of sports writing by either Tom Van Dycke (under the name of Dave Farrell) or a new staff member, Lou Seligson, Seligson was a hard-hitting young sports writer. He also covered trials and city hall and whatever other assignments turned up.

Al decided to run a column of Woody's work. It was called "Woody Sez" and frequently ran on the front page of the paper. I'm sure that Al was under considerable pressure. It must have been difficult for him to use that material, particularly on the front page. The general attitude of the top leadership of the Party was that the paper ought to be much more dignified, serious, and pretty rigidly political. Quite a few leaders felt that the space for things like "Woody Sez" or for Mike Quinn's column, one of the really fine features of the paper and extremely popular, were a waste of good editorial space. Mike Quinn's column was later collected into a book called *Dangerous Thoughts*, a unique collection of satire, wonderful stories, all strongly socialist. In our time, Arthur Hoppe, who writes for the *San Francisco Chronicle*, comes close to Mike's style. Woody's columns, "Woody Sez," were collected into an attractive book that was published in 1975 under the same title as the column.

His column was introduced on the front page of the paper in a big spread that included his brief autobiography:

Woody Sez, p. 10.

WOODY SEZ: *A New Col* *Introduces*

Woorow Guthrie or just plain Woody as he is known to thousands of radio listeners, will be a daily feature in The People's World from now on.

Woody calls himself a hill-billy singer. He is one of the 200,000 people who came from the dustbowl looking for work and a little food—the people who have picked the fruit and the crops of California—lived in shanty camps, been beaten and driven about by the bank-landowners.

But Woody came with a guitar on his back and with an eye and an ear sensitive to the suffering of his own people.

He sings songs every day over KFVD from 2:15 to 2:45 and has many thousands of listeners and people who write him letters. He writes these songs himself.

And Woody has gathered a great deal of homely wisdom from his people. Each day he will speak to you on this page in his own way about how he looks at things.

But just to introduce Woody to you, we've asked him to tell us about himself and this is what he sends.

Here's Woody's biography:

AWTOWBYOGRAFIE

Well, I was born in Okemah, Okfuskee County, Oklahoma, in 1912, the year that Woodrow Wilson was nominated for President. My dad was quite a figger in Okfuskee county politics at that time, an' so he named me after the President, Woodrow Wilson Guthrie—which is too much of a name for a country boy! So I sawed off all the fancy work an' jest left "Woody"—I cood remember that.

Okemah got to be a oil boom town, just like about ½ the other towns down there, an' got to be full of boom-chasers, drillers, roustabouts, tool-dressers, teamskinners, bootleggers, Indian guardians, an' other tong-buckers an' grease monkeys of the oil field work. When Okemah went dead, I left town with the first migration, headed for the plains of west Texas, around Amarillo, Pampa, and Borger.

I worked several years in a drug store which turned into a likker store when prohibition went out. The boss of the likker store said that on that very day I took a greater liking to my work. Personal, I woodent say. Anyhow, in them oil boom towns, located as they was right in the big middle of the dust bowl, it was dern hard to find a place of business that wasn't engaged directly or indirectly in the bootleg game.

MATRIMONY

You know when the [illegible] weather both set in [illegible] ain't nothin' else to do [illegible]

An, you know, when [illegible] faith in old mammy [illegible]

Well, I married a girl [illegible] them days. She was the [illegible] a family of Oklahoma [illegible] down around Hydro. [illegible] been married six or [illegible] shore)—but have got [illegible] an Baby Sue, 1½.

HANDY MAN

We wrestled with the [illegible] Texas till we wore the [illegible] it clean, an' finally [illegible] ground hogs for a [illegible]

I worked as a grocery [illegible] ner painter, windo [illegible] around clean-up man.

I got what you [illegible] rooled me up a bunch of [illegible] tall, frate-train that [illegible] side of it. I got down [illegible] "reefer"--somewhere in [illegible] daylight I seen, it said [illegible] below sea level.

ROVING MAN

I was a headin' out [illegible] didn't know for shore [illegible] a livin' under, so you [illegible] tically without a [illegible] didn't know where the [illegible]

So when the police [illegible] —I jest asked 'em where [illegible] wus, un' hooked up, an' [illegible] you can rest easy [illegible] goin' nowheres in the [illegible]

I'd jest stand out by the [illegible] thumbs up, an' [illegible] ternal to me. I didn't [illegible]

RADIO HIT

Anyway, I seen some [illegible] great senery, from the [illegible] forests, from Reno, all [illegible] bay. I finally fooled around [illegible] up at Turlock, Calif, so [illegible] picked up an' name was [illegible] w've been ever since

I was asked here a while [illegible] ever git started on the [illegible] I don't know. I jest went [illegible] office, an' I says, how come [illegible] Okay, and so, with other [illegible] musicians who done sung [illegible]

Ed Robbin and Byron Dunham was having somewhat of a gentlemenly argument about some high-fangled terms — about the various planes or phases of consciousness one goes through (in becoming plumb conscious) among others of which they talked of class consciousness.

Now Ed and Byron was plumb out of my territory a using them high falutin' words, but I enjoyed the consciousness as much as they did.

I walked into the room where they was, an' Byron, he up and says, "Now you take Woody here, he ain't a bit class conscious, are you, Woody?"

An' Ed says, "Why, shore, he's class conscious — why you woodent know a class conscious feller if you met him in the road."

And then they asked me, "What do you think policemen is hired to do, pertect rich folks property, or safeguard the widows an orphens?"

And I says, "Well, what few policemen I ever knowed — they was more or less hired — I reckon to pertect rich folks property — and then the widows and orphens, too."

Woody Sez, p. 14

Forum

I STARTED A SUNDAY NIGHT FORUM in connection with my program. I rented a small hall and invited speakers or arranged debates or simply had current events discussions with audience participation. Sometimes I brought *People's World* editor Al Richmond or a writer and speaker who covered foreign affairs, such as John Pittman from the paper or anybody else who could shed some light on the politics of the time. Frequently I would ask Woody to come to the forum to sing his songs and lighten the atmosphere. The big problem with Woody was getting him off the stage. He loved to drawl out long commentaries and tell endless anecdotes between his songs, and it practically took a hook to pull him off the platform.

I had a friend, George Shibley, who was ready to speak or debate whenever I needed him. He was a brilliant young labor lawyer, who represented the labor unions of the Long Beach and San Pedro waterfront arena and was well informed about labor politics. Shibley was of Arab descent and was deeply interested in the politics of the Middle East. When he came to the forum, he and I would go round and round on the Israeli–Arab situation. I had lived in Israel during the late twenties and early thirties and was concerned with the development of the Jewish state. Shibley was very pro-Arab. So we had heated but friendly discussions. It was possible then to talk about that situation and still remain friends. We were even able to be humorous in our debate. All this was long before the holocaust, which destroyed six million Jews and sent tens of thousands of survivors to Israel.

Fortunately for me, the hierarchy of the Communist party did not attend these forums. If they had, I probably would have been reprimanded, because even then the Party's attitude toward the Jewish state was not friendly. Much has happened since those days forty years ago. In 1948 Israel became a state and has since fought several wars in which many thousands of both Jews and Arabs have died. But the whole Middle East situation is as unresolved as it was when Shibley and I were debating.

I remember a forum when things got really hot between us. He maintained that the Jews had no place in the Middle East — that this was Arab land the Jews were stealing, and that the Jews were being used as imperialist pawns. I went into the historic right of the Jews to this small plot of earth, and said that Jews had bought and paid for the land they occupied. The debate that night got somewhat bitter. So I called a halt and asked Woody to sing some songs. As he tuned his guitar, he started talking in his slow drawl: "I don't know much about the politics in those countries way across the seas, and I don't know whether Ed or George is right. But I got a song that says it all, because wherever there are people, the struggle is much the same. It

ain't nation and nation or one color and another. It's always
been the rich squeezing the poor. And it's the same in those
lands where the prophets from Isaiah to Jesus preached the
same thing." Then he sang:

> *Jesus Christ was a man who traveled through the land,*
> *A hard-working man and brave.*
> *He said to the rich*
> *Give your goods to the poor,*
> *But they put Jesus Christ in his grave.*
> *Jesus was a man,*
> *A carpenter by hand,*
> *His followers true and brave.*
> *One dirty little coward called Judas Iscariot*
> *Has laid Jesus Christ in his grave.*
> *When Jesus come to town,*
> *The working folk around*
> *Believed what he did say.*
> *Bankers and the preachers,*
> *They nailed him to the cross,*
> *And they laid Jesus Christ in his grave©.*

Those were Woody's "politics." It didn't matter whether he
was talking about Harlan County, Jerusalem, Oklahoma, or
Cairo. He didn't bother to read what Karl Marx had written, or
Lenin. Woody believed that what is important is the struggle of
the working people to win back the earth, which is rightfully
theirs. He believed that people should love one another and
organize into one big union. That's the way he saw politics and
world affairs.

As for Shibley, years later he got involved in a case in Long
Beach where he represented a Marine who had been sentenced
to the brig for some alleged crime. Shibley took the case for
appeal and attempted to subpoena the Navy records. They refused to allow him to see the records but Shibley obtained them
somehow.

◄ Woody picking cotton at Woodpatch, California, 1939. Courtesy Marjorie Guthrie.

He won the case for the Marine, who was exonerated and released, but Shibley was arrested and charged with having obtained the records illegally and went to jail where he served a three-year sentence.

In recent years, Shibley became further involved in the Arab cause. He represented Sirhan Sirhan in the early days of that case. I do not see Shibley now. Our paths are far apart. Will they cross again someday in the future?

Woody in the Kean River. Courtesy Marjorie Guthrie. ▼

I've got a high feeling runnin' in me
About a good book done well,
And I've actually wrote up some of the longest, hottest
Pages and stacks of pages in the forms of novels and true
*   tales,*
But still there is something too slow and too plowy and
*   ploddy*
For me to spend my time at following around with long
*   novels*
When I'd rather to hear a room full of my comrades and
*   friends*
Sing out real loud on one of my songs
Which I've wrote, say, from start to finish
So before I turn out my lights to call it a night
Let me just leave you with this plain in your head
That I've never heard nobody yet get a whole room full
Of friends and enemies both
To sing and ring the plaster down singing out a novel
Like I've heard them sing out my songs already.

Born to Win, pp. 28–29

Dreiser

LATE IN 1939 Theodore Dreiser called to tell me how much he liked one of my programs. Dreiser had been one of my literary gods since my teens, so I was flattered and excited.

I asked Dreiser whether I could come and see him, and he urged me to do that. He lived in Hollywood at the time, I think on Kings Road, with his wife Helen, a beautiful reddish-haired woman. A few days later I stopped by the modest stucco house just below Santa Monica Boulevard and knocked at his door.

We talked about politics and the world, and I asked Dreiser whether he would be willing to let me interview him for my program.

"I'll do it if you will write the interview. You know what I think."

I knew that he hated the British, particularly British imperialism, and that he was strongly pro-labor and against war. So I focused the interview on these themes. Dreiser liked what I did so well that he had the interview beautifully printed and sent it out to a private mailing list.

On that first visit I remarked on the huge and very lovely desk in the front room where he worked.

"This desk is rosewood," said Dreiser. "It was made from a grand piano that belonged to my brother, Paul Dreiser. He left it

to me when he died and I had this desk made. I take it with me
wherever I go.

Woody as he looked in the late 1930s. Courtesy Woody Guthrie Publications. ▼

"Paul was the songwriter who wrote "My Gal Sal." Yes, that and a hundred other tunes. He was my favorite brother. I cared very much about him."

I told Dreiser about Woody. Then I invited him and Helen to come to our house for dinner and said I'd ask Woody to come over to join us and sing some songs.

The day of the dinner arrived. My wife, Clara, had made a great pot of chicken paprikash. She probably would have had the whole Guthrie family to dinner if I had permitted it. Clara has always managed to have a bottomless pot. If five or six extra people arrive unexpectedly, they are immediately invited to dinner and somehow the food is there. This has always been true, whether we have been rich or poor. The miracle of the loaves and fishes has been repeated a thousand times in our household.

But this time I did not want a crowd, at least not early in the evening. I had envisioned a literary evening in which I would question Dreiser about people like Sherwood Anderson, Frank Norris, and H. L. Mencken, all of whom had been his friends and colleagues. Well, it wasn't to be that kind of evening at all.

Dreiser and Helen were right on time. Dreiser was so big he practically filled our small living room. He had a strong face and head, rough and unfinished, a large, slow-moving hulk of a man with power and stubbornness written all over him.

At the table, where Dreiser ate heartily and remarked at how close the paprikash was to his German mother's cooking, most of the conversation was between my son Dan and Dreiser. Dan was a serious, mature ten-year-old, and adults took to him immediately. Dreiser questioned him about school, his friends, what kind of books he read, how he spent his time after school. You would have thought he was writing a treatise on children. And both Dreiser and his wife were charmed by our little girl Tamara, then about four, who prattled, sang, danced, and showed off whenever she could squeeze into what was going on.

After dinner Woody wandered in from next door. I had asked him to bring his guitar and sing some songs. I still remember some of the conversation because I was amused by how it began.

Theodore Dreiser said, "Ed's been telling me about your songs, but I don't think I've caught you on the radio."

"Then we start even, Mr. Dreiser, 'cause I ain't read any of your books."

Woody sang some of the dust bowl ballads. Dreiser, I remember, was particularly interested in what a dust storm looked like and how people reacted.

"It looked like the end of the world," said Woody. As he described it, suddenly the sun was covered over. A black cloud would appear on the horizon. People would start scurrying for their homes or crowd into the churches. Then this black dust would sweep through the streets and it seemed as if the whole town was whirling in darkness. Woody and his folks crowded into their house, trying to fill every crack and cranny with rags and paper to keep the dust out. "I seen people praying and shouting hallelujah."

But after it was over and the town started sweeping and shaking off the dust that covered everything, that's when the real trouble started. People got used to the wind and the dust. But they never could get used to what it did to their lives—the dirt of their farms blowing away, farmers sinking deeper and deeper into debt and poverty, families breaking up, and their neighbors, one by one, trundling off in old jalopies with families and furniture, looking for a place where they could make a living.

Dreiser talked about how he was raised in Indiana, Terre Haute and Warsaw, how he'd been part of a large family. He told about the tornadoes he'd seen in Indiana when he was a boy. He talked about the struggle his family had gone through to keep alive, how he'd gone out to pick up wood and coal at the railroad track to have some warmth through the long winters.

Dreiser and Woody found much in common in a similar kind of childhood impoverishment.

Then Dreiser mentioned his brother Paul, who had changed his name to Dresser and become a famous songwriter. Woody knew and played "My Gal Sal." And Dreiser mentioned that he had written the words for one song to Paul's music at Paul's behest—"On the Banks of the Wabash." The chorus went:

Oh the moonlight's fair tonight along the Wabash,
From the fields there comes the breath of new mown hay.
Through the sycamores the candlelights are gleaming,
On the banks of the Wabash far away. ©

Then my daughter Tammy snuggled up to Woody and said she wanted to sing a song.

She sang "Put Your Finger on Your Nose, on Your Nose."

Soon everyone was singing to Woody's guitar and putting their fingers on their noses and on their ears and on their toes.

Then the evening was over and we hadn't talked about literature or Anderson, Norris, or Mencken, but everyone had had a good meal and a good time.

Life has got a habit of not standing hitched. You got to ride it like you find it. You got change with it. If a day goes by that don't change some of your old notions for new ones, that is just about like trying to milk a dead cow.

Woody Sez, p. 166

Ackerman

I GUESS ALL RADICAL newspapers are plagued with business types who want to help them popularize their papers. The *People's World* was no exception. Shortly after I met Woody, a man named Buck Ackerman came in to see me at the office. The conversation ensued that went something like this:

"Ed, I listen to your program pretty regularly and I'm a subscriber to your paper."

"That's good."

"No, it's not good."

"Why?"

"What kind of response do you get to the program?"

I pointed to a pile of letters on the desk. "See for yourself. Most of these letters have subscriptions to the paper or testimony to help the program. What do you think of the program, Mr. Ackerman?"

"Do you want to know the truth?"

"Of course."

"It stinks. That's what I think."

"What's the matter with it?"

"Have you got time to go out for a cup of coffee and the best pancakes in Los Angeles?"

"Mr. Ackerman, I'm the Los Angeles editor of this paper. I write a daily column. There are only two of us to cover all the news of the city and besides that, now I have a daily radio program of news commentary to write. Do you think I have time to go out and have pancakes?"

"That's what's wrong with your program, and probably with your paper," said Ackerman, looking at me over his glasses. He had a drooping lip, a dour look, and a long, red nose, and he wore a beat-up fedora hat.

That was my first meeting with Buck, and though I took a raincheck on that pancake session, he didn't give up. He came by every few days to drag me out of the office, always with the bait of buying me pancakes or an ice cream soda. Someone must have told him how vulnerable I was to those particular goodies.

Woody, too, used to drop in, and we'd go to lunch or coffee or just fiddle around the office. He loved to bang on the typewriter, and he'd usually wind up with a song or two.

Well, about the third or fourth Ackerman visit, I succumbed to the bribe. Woody was in the office and I introduced him to Buck, who invited Woody to come along.

"In the first place I'm going to take you for the best pancakes around, and second, I got something to say to you, too, Woody Guthrie. You ain't no stranger to me because I hear your songs on KFVD and I agree with Ed that you're a poet. You're my kind of guy. You're talking to the people that count."

So we piled into Buck's new Ford. He drove us out to a place on Wilshire Boulevard. There we ordered stacks of very thin pancakes and coffee. Finally Buck started on me.

"Ed, I'm a retired businessman. I'm not a rich man, mind you, but I got enough to last my days. I made it with a patent medicine mail order business. I'm just giving you my credentials, you understand."

"I understand."

"I've been a supporter of the movement for many years, even back in New York where I come from. Now I'm retired and I'm going to take it easy. I could just go to you people and give you a couple of thousand dollars to salve my conscience, but that isn't what I want to do. I want to apply the principles I used to build my business to help your business, our business. Our business is to sell socialism to the American people. Are you with me?"

"I'm with you, Buck. So what am I doing wrong?"

"You just listen to Woody real good and you'll figure it out for yourself."

"But I like Ed's program. I'm learnin' a lot just listenin' to what he says on the air," said Woody.

"I'm not talking about what he says. What he says is important. But it's the way it's done. You've got to talk to people as though you were sitting in a room with them, maybe across a kitchen table, the way we're talking right now. That's what Woody does. You hear him on the radio and you know he's just talking to his own folks about the things that matter to them. That's what you've got to do on your program, Ed. Make the news interesting and dramatic, but tell it to people in an intimate way, as though you were sitting in their kitchen over a cup of coffee."

I listened attentively to Buck. He was a shrewd man. I had been trying to feel my way into the kind of commentary he was talking about, simple, down-to-earth talk about the meaning and the background of the news. After my session with Buck, whenever I was on the air I visualized someone sitting across from me, and I talked to that person. It had to be someone I liked, to make it warm and friendly. I know it worked because I began to get a lot of mail response.

Buck turned to Woody.

"In my case," said Woody, as he poured some more boysenberry juice on a last pancake, "it's not a cup of coffee but a bottle of wine we're passing around as we sit around a fire in a squatter's camp, singing songs and exchanging tales."

"Woody," said Buck, "you do your stuff and then send out mimeographed copies of some of your songs, and people send you mostly quarters. Is that so?"

"That's just about it, Buck. Though I sometimes get some tattered dollar bills."

"Well, I think we should make up nice printed copies of your songs and sayings and peddle them for a dollar. You could sell them over the air and take a bunch of them along to sell at all these gatherings where you play."

"I've got nothing against all that exceptin' those printers want to be paid and I ain't got what it takes."

"I've got a friend who owns a print shop and could do a real good job," I said.

"I'll gladly put up the money," said Buck, "if it isn't over $50."

There was a print shop called the Plantin Press. It was owned by Saul Marks and his wife Lillian. Their shop was on the gound floor of the frame house they lived in on the corner of Santa Monica and Sunset Boulevards. Saul was an exceptional printer. He took great pride in his craft and was doing a lot of printing for various left-wing organizations. He had been telling me that he really wanted to do pamphlets and books. So when we arrived that same afternoon and asked him to do an attractive small pamphlet of Woody's songs, he was glad to oblige and to do it at a minimal cost.

This, I thought, was the first printed publication of Woody's songs. The pamphlets helped Woody to increase his income. Unfortunately, I don't save things, so I don't have a copy.

Woody was canny and sometimes secretive. As far as I can remember, he did not mention to Buck or to me that he (or KFVD) had already put out a little paper booklet of his songs and comments and they had run out of copies. Just recently I ran across a copy of that booklet.

WOODY AND LEFTY LOU'S
FAVORITE COLLECTION

Old Time
Hill Country
Songs

Being Sung for Ages
Still Going Strong

Cover of Woody's first song collection. ▲

Lefty Lou, with whom Woody had been singing on KFVD and around the countryside, had dropped out of the program before I met Woody. Her real name was Maxine Crissman. Many of the songs in the KFVD booklet were written with Lefty.

At the end of each song Woody wrote a comment like the ones he was to develop later in the column "Woody Sez." The songs were not yet political. For the most part they were transformed old folk tunes. Many were love songs or work songs.

I'm a-takin' it easy,
I'm a-takin' it slow.
And I ain't gonna worry,
No mo', no mo'.

Worked so hard in a kafi cornfield,
I wore blisters on my heel,
I sat down in the shade of a tree,
Sally come along and said to me [chorus].

Down in the cotton patch half way round,
I'd done picked a hundred pound.
Pulled my sack to the end of the row,
Says, Now, Sal, I thought you knowed [chorus].

I love a gal on a certain street,
Purty little gal, sho' is sweet,
Ten years we have set and set,
I ain't never told her yet [chorus].©

Near the end of the booklet, Woody commented: "That's one the kids like. It was borned over in Glendale. But all through our program you will feel us trying to get you to take it easy and drop your work a little while to rest and listen to some slow, old, easygoing songs."

Then there was a page under the heading "Woody," which is so typical of the way he loved to ramble between songs in all his performances that I think it's worth printing.

WOODY

Well, when I go to write about myself, I cain't say much, 'cause I ain't got no material to work on. I've been around the country fer years, a Hobo Hillbilly, eating about twice a week whether I was hungry or not. I've worked in a lot of places, but never did have anybody write and tell me that my work was a bright spot in their day till I got on the air waves in front of a microbephone. I never did drink anything stronger than water for a chaser, and never spend my money foolish unless I'm by myself or with somebody. I am a believer in everybody and everything, extry modern, and extry old fashioned. My contract with KFVD don't give me enough money to get the bighead, but it gives me enough that I don't care what other people think about me. I'm just a pore boy tryin' to get along. The dust run me out of Texas, and the Officers run me in at Lincoln Heights. But they was nice to me. They had bars fixed up over the windows so nobody could get in and steal my guitar. I was hijacking on credit till I got on the radio. Now I plan to put in a second hand bank. I am never surprised or disappointed, for I have no regret or future ambitions. I am a lazy man, and cain't help it. Ugly and cain't fix it. The Universe is my home, and Los Angeles is just a vase in my parlor. I don't care if school keeps or not. I like pore people because they'll come out winner in the long run. And I like rich people because they need friendship.

If Roosevelt wants to count the population in Los Angeles, he'd better git started before smudge pot season opens up, or it'll be so black around here he cain't find the people.

If Mr. and Mrs. Wally Simpson would go Hillbilly, they wouldn't be bothered by Cameramen, especially if they needed a haircut as bad as I do.

A cigar box is a handy thing to have in the house when a thing of that kind is needed.

Can you think of a thing in this world that is known for certain? I cain't. Why argue then about educations?

Woody and Lefty Lou, when Woody first started doing a show at KFVD in Los ▲ Angeles.

I'm blowin' down this old dusty road;
Yes, I'm blowin' down this old dusty road;
I'm blowin' down this old dusty road, Lord God,
And I ain't a-gonna be treated this a-way.©

Woody Guthrie Folk Songs, p. 75

The Guthrie Family Descends on Us

SOMETIME IN 1939, Woody took off for New York. He had been persuaded by Will Geer that he ought to meet Pete Seeger and other folk singers. He sent Mary and the children back to Texas and told them to wait there for him.

While Woody was in New York, he hooked up with Pete and formed the Almanac Singers. It was at this time that he met Alan Lomax and was invited to Washington, D.C., to record his folk songs and anecdotes for the Library of Congress. Woody also had a brief commercial success in New York, when he got on one of the big networks. But he couldn't take the commercialism and soon walked out.

Woody did make enough money for a payment on a new Buick. Then he left New York, drove to Texas and picked up Mary and the children, and hightailed it for Los Angeles.

And so it was that one rainy night at about 2 A.M. Woody knocked at our door. He and the family had been traveling for days, and they needed a place to stay. They all looked miserable, tired and cold. Clara fed everybody and bedded them down. In the morning I saw that the big new car was already beat up, with bent fenders and broken windows. The family had been living in it as they came across the country, and Woody had never been a respecter of property, particularly property that belonged to the finance company. Looking at the car, I remembered him singing:

I've been through some hard traveling,
I thought you knowed.
I've been having some hard traveling,
Way down the road.

Our house was very small. The only bedroom was a tiny room with bunk beds for our two kids. My wife and I had been sleeping on a couch in the living room. And now Woody's family had arrived. For the next few days there were grown-ups and children spread all over the floors on blankets and mattresses.

There was a shanty next door owned by a shrunken old lady in her eighties, Mrs. Wolfson, who had moved away to Pasadena. Mrs. Wolfson had been on the Yiddish stage many years before, and she spoke in a hoarse guttural voice. She loved to recite passages from the melodramas she had played in. She also wrote poetry, some of it which she had paid to have published. I remember one that went something like this:

Roses are Red
Violets are Blue
I hate Hitler
And so should you.

The sentiment expressed was enough to endear her to me, although she was one of the ugliest women I have ever seen.

I mentioned to Woody that the cottage next door was vacant and that we could take a trip out to Pasadena to find out whether it was available.

"You mean it's empty?"

"She's been out of there a couple of months."

"Well, let's get going," said Woody.

I thought he meant get going to Pasadena to see the old lady. But within the next hour Woody had pried open a window and moved his family into the house. Then we went around to my friends, rustling up furniture and dishes and generally trying to make the place livable. It was a couple of months before I was able to prod Woody into making the trip to Pasadena to see the old lady and get her permission to rent the house.

We traveled out there together, and I introduced Woody to Mrs. Wolfson. She was living in a small, neat apartment, with flower boxes on the windows and a frazzled one-eyed cat for a companion. I told her that Woody and his family needed a place to live. And Woody started strumming on his guitar and singing some of his songs. The old lady was completely taken by him, particularly when she showed him her own rhymes and he started to put them to music and sing them for her. I guess by the

---

Woody, Mary, and their three kids—Sue, Billy, and Gwen—sitting on the stoop of the cottage next door to us on Preston Street in Los Angeles, 1940. Courtesy Marjorie Guthrie.▼

time he was through she would have given him the house. They settled on his paying a rent of ten dollars a month, so his new home was legal—though he never did pay the ten dollars.

Meantime, Woody was worried about the Buick, which he had bought in New York. He owed the finance company most of the cost, because he had made only one payment. The car was already half a wreck.

Sure enough the finance company finally nailed him and took the car away. That night Woody got very drunk and started throwing beer bottles through the windows of the house. The kids came over to our house with his wife Mary, and they huddled there all through the night. By morning the storm was over and Woody was his old gentle self. Just a few busted windows and broken bottles to take care of.

This incident was an exception, however. Most of Woody's time in the cottage was spent productively. It was there that he started to write *Bound for Glory*, which he completed later, in New York.

His writing was unedited, uncensored, uncritical. But it was Woody, his own searching, feeling, probing, singing self, reaching out to touch people, children, things, to understand and simplify. You read patches of *Born to Win*, a collection of Woody's writings, and you want to skip some of the long, rambling sections because they seem too simplistic. But then you come back, because they're like the green grass or like dandelions in a field, or clover, common and sweet smelling. Maybe all this is what makes him a folk poet. Nothing is precious. It all springs from roots that are common to all human experience.

And so when he sat down to write *Bound for Glory* in the cottage next door, I would hear that typewriter going like a riveting machine, all hours of the day or night. He needed no privacy, no view, no special conditions conducive to writing. The kids were in and out of the house and Mary was in the kitchen cooking, or out playing with the children, and Woody just pounded away at the typewriter while the pages piled up on the side of the kitchen table.

Woody was tireless. That wiry little fellow was all energy. I don't know when he slept. Perhaps that's why he would take catnaps during the meetings where he was scheduled to play. He would pound the typewriter all day, play at a party at night. And then when the party shut down, he would frequently go to a bar on Skid Row, Fifth Street east of Main in Los Angeles. Sometimes I went along to see what it was like. Those bars were crowded with migrant workers in from the farms or waiting for work. Woody would wander in with his guitar hung around his neck, and immediately there were people who knew him.

"Hey, Woody, how's the music business? Here's the old Woody—comes from my town, Okemah. How's the family, Woody? Here y'ar, Woody—have a drink and give us a song."

Then Woody would drink wine or beer and sing and play until the bar closed.

These were his people and the people who listened to him on the radio. He exchanged tales with them about what had happened back home in Oklahoma, Texas, Arkansas, or Tennessee. His songs were made up of the warp and woof of their lives, the hard times in the field, and the boom times in the oil fields. This was Woody's best audience.

I've read a big mountain of books, both good and bad, on the subject of the soul, the heart, the spirit, the mind of man, but I've not stumbled in my labors so far upon any one medicine (that has not already been discovered and fairly well named and branded before I got to be born).

Love is the only medicine that I believe in. It enters into all other forms of good medicine and good nursing. To me the easy rub and gentle touch of the nursing hand is more potent and longer lasting in its healing powers than all or any other known drug medicine.

Love is the only God that I'll ever believe in©.

Born to Win, p. 164

64

Of Love
and Latkes

EVERYTHING IS INTERCONNECTED. Pick up a thread any place and follow it, and eventually it will lead you back home.

For example, what possible connection can there be between potato latkes and Woody Guthrie? Well, for one thing I just today discovered that Woody once wrote a Hanukah song about latkes, the traditional food for that holiday. It went:

> *How many latkes can you eat?*
> *It's Hanukah.*
> *How many Latkes can you eat?*
> *It's Hanukah.*
> *How many Latkes can you eat?*
> *It's ten times threeth good and bad, on the subject of the soul, the heart, the spirit, the mind of man, but I've not stumbled in my labors so far upon any one medicine (that has not already been discovered and fairly well named and branded before I got to be born).*
> *undermen six times eight.*
> *It's Hanukah.*
> *Yes, Yes, It's Hanukah.*©

About a year ago I went to a Hanukah latke party at the big old home of a communal group in Berekely. The usual Berkeley crowd—doctors, lawyers, social workers, writers, artists, plumbers, painters, young and old, and a sprinkling of musicians with their guitars, banjos, or flutes, sitting in the corners and fingering their instruments.

Having eaten my fill of crisp, delicious latkes, I picked up a conversation with a good-looking friendly woman and told her that I was trying to write this book of memoirs. I mentioned that my memory is so poor I was having trouble scratching up things that had happened many years ago.

"How curious that you should talk to me about this. I'm a hypnotist and I've been specializing in helping writers who are blocked," she said. Then she told me that she had written a book of self-hypnosis and that it would appear shortly.

In his later writing, Woody wrote some of the best erotic prose of the time. So I had been wondering why I could not remember his talking to me about his love life. Then I found the book written by Freda Morris, the latke party lady. I read it and tried hypnotizing myself. It did evoke a day that I had long forgotten.

That day I had decided to follow my friend Buck Ackerman's advice—to get away from the office once in a while and take a fresh look at what I was doing. I picked up Woody at his house and we set out for a day at the beach.

In those days smog had not yet yellowed and smothered Los Angeles. It was a shining, sunny day late in February of 1940. The air was sparkling, clear, and I decided to take the long way out Sunset Strip to Santa Monica and the sea. Going through Beverly Hills and Brentwood, we drove past the palatial estates of the millionaires and movie stars. Woody, who had not been through this part of the county before, started a conversation, which I remember somewhat like this:

"I don't see no cotton or beans growing 'round here. Just lots of green, green, green ... all bucks ... all the do re mi in the world."

"Woody, think you'd like to live in one of those mansions? Your kids would have lots of fun playing on the lawns."

"Ed," he said, "I have lots of dreams and fancies, but that's not one of them. I'd rather sleep in a barn or a hobo jungle than in one of those posh palaces. Don't think I was ever meant to be royalty.... But those places are mighty pretty ... mighty pretty."

We drove clear down to the sea and then north toward

Malibu, parked the car and decided to walk. Woody took off his boots and turned up his trousers. I did the same, and we walked in the surf. I must have told Woody of some romantic involvement of my own, because I recall that then he told me this tale.

"People think that hoboin' and knocking around the country is full of adventure and that you're always meetin' up with women. It ain't that way. It's lonesome and dirty and full of hard knocks. It's gettin' throwed in jail and gettin' beat up and goin' hungry and sometimes findin' a friend for a short time.

"But one time somethin' happened to me that comes back now. I'd been ridin' the rails followin' the crops and I dropped off a freight in a small town in the Imperial Valley. Strange I can't even remember the name of the town, and I thought I'd never forget it.

"I was dirty, tired, and hungry, and I didn't have a nickel for a beer. Always found if you have to hustle a meal, stay away from the wealthier sections of town. . . . Go to the places where the workers live, because they been hungry and they're likely to share a mite.

"Tried a few houses, small frame houses that were on the outskirts of the town, and no one was home. Then I tried a couple asking if there was any odd jobs I could do and I got turned away, but kindly, not mean.

"I was mighty hot, tired, and discouraged, and I was going to give up. Thought I'd give it one more try. This was a white house with a neat fence and gate and no dog. Also the front door was open, so I walked up and knocked. Figured the lady was back in the kitchen and didn't hear me. I went around the back. There she was diggin' around a vegetable garden.

"She was on her knees loosening the earth around some tomato plants . . . a nice looking woman about thirty. She kinda brushed her hair back from her forehead and asked me what I wanted."

"'I'm mighty handy with a paint brush or a shovel,' I said, 'and I need a little work because I'm downright hungry.'

"She got up from her knees, walked over and give me a good look."

"'God, you're dirty,' she said, 'How'd you get that dirty?'"

"'Just rode in on a freight train and the accommodations ain't exactly commodious.' She looked a little doubtful so I said,

'If you ain't got no work for me I could play you some music. I haven't got my guitar with me but I got this harmonica and I'd play some real nice tunes.'"

Woody and I wandered over to a large rock under a cliff and dropped down onto the sand. For a few moments we watched a fishing boat creeping along the blue sea a couple hundred yards from the shore.

"C'mon Woody, don't leave me hung up in the middle of this tale. What happened?"

"Well, when I said I was a music man, that changed things. She said to come right into the kitchen and she'd fix me some breakfast and not to worry about the work or music for a while."

"What did she look like, Woody?"

"Well, she wasn't what you'd call a beauty. A kind of plain, friendly-looking woman with a full, shapely body. A face that had some freckles, very young, kind of boyish looking. Brownish black hair put up in a loose bun with straggly bits over her forehead and real blue-green eyes . . . I saw all this later, because just then I was thinking of one thing and that was food."

"The kitchen was clean and everything was in place. A pot of coffee was simmering on the stove. I felt embarrassed sitting down in my dirty clothes and with my hands and face grimy."

"'Go on, wash up . . . take a bath if you like,' she said, 'while I rustle up some food.'

"I sure took her at her word, filled the tub with hot water and scrubbed down. After a little she came to the door and said, 'Here's an old robe. Bring out your clothes and we'll see if I can clean them for you. Help yourself to the bath towels and breakfast is on the table.'

"So I dried myself, put on the robe, which was much too big for me, and took my clothes out with me. I pulled my harmonica out of my pocket and stuck it in the pocket of the robe. Shoved my clothes in a bundle in the washroom by the porch and then went into the kitchen. That lady had sure laid out some grub — eggs and sausage and muffins, to say nothing of the marmalade, coffee, and some tomatoes from her garden. What a feast — I hardly knew what to say.

"'Go to it,' she said, 'I've already eaten, but I'm going to have some coffee and keep you company. First off we haven't introduced ourselves. I'm Kate.'

Dust Bowl Refugee

Words and Music by Woody Guthrie

Sauntering steadily

mp smoothly

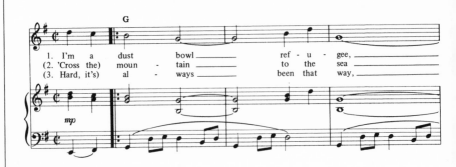

G

1. I'm a dust bowl ref - u - gee, ____
(2. 'Cross the) moun - tain ____ to the sea ____
(3. Hard, it's) al - ways ____ been that way,

mp

D7

____ Just a dust bowl ____ ref - u - gee. ____
Come the wife and ____ kids and me. ____
Here to - day and ____ on our way.

86

"'I'm Woody Guthrie,' I said. 'I come from Oklahoma and I'm out here followin' the crops when I'm not makin' music.'

"'Eat your fill, Woody Guthrie,' she said. 'It's been a while since I had a man to feed so I enjoy it. I'm a widow. My husband was killed in the Kentucky mines a few years ago and I been out here since then.'

"'No kids?' I asked.

"'No, just myself to care for. You're lucky to have found me home. I'm a bookkeeper in a warehouse and just decided to take the day off. I get awful tired of working in an office every day, so I just stayed home sick and if they don't like it they know what they can do.'

"'My lucky day,' I said, still gobbling down the food. 'Guess we were just fated to meet at a breakfast table.'

"When I finished eating I pulled the harmonica out of my pocket and started playing some way out tunes while she took my clothes and stuffed them in the washtub.

"Then she came back and took me to the living room. It was real comfortable, with a big overstuffed brown sofa, a rocker that looked like she must have brought it with her from back East. On the mantle was a large photograph of a husky, smiling man.

"'That was my husband Harry. He was killed in a mine accident in Kentucky. That was more than two years ago.'

"'This his robe I'm wearin'?'

"'Yes . . . a little big on you,' she laughed.

"I sat down on the couch and Kate sat on the rocker, listening while I played some tunes on the harmonica. Then I started singing some of my songs and playing the harmonica between verses. Played 'I'm blowin' down this old dusty road' and some of the other dust bowl ballads and pretty soon she had slipped down to the floor and was leanin' against my knee. There's nothing like singing to bring a woman to you . . . so I just kept on singin' and then in felt her hand slip through the robe to touch my leg. I didn't want to make any wrong move to a woman who'd treated me so kind, but soon, I have to tell you, that robe was standing up like a tent right there in the middle, and then Kate said,

"'I hope you won't think I'm too forward, Woody, but I sure like you and I been alone in this little town for two years without a man....'

"I leaned over and kissed her and then slipped to the floor to embrace her. But after a little huggin' and kissin' she said, 'Let's do this right, Woody. I want to be in bed with you....'

"She took me to the bedroom that had a blue cover on the bed and tucked me under the sheets and then went to the bathroom to get ready. She come out naked and slipped in beside me. I threw the covers off so I could take a good look at her and she didn't play no games nor show any false modesty. She let me take my fill of looking. I'm a man that loves tits and hers were just full and ripe and I ran my hand real slow all over her body right down to her feet. I nestled my head in that full reddish bush, kissed her soft belly, sucked her breasts and then stretched out beside her and let her take her fill of looking me over and feeling and kissing me very softly all over. I guess we both had this feeling of very hungry people who suddenly have a feast before them and want to look at it and smell it and savor it before they dig in.... At least that's the way it was with me. And then we made love on and off all through the day, talking and loving and getting to know each other slowly and deeply.

"Then Kate brought back my clothes, which she had found time to hang dry between our love sessions. Toward evening I'd dressed and we had some supper. After that Kate insisted on giving me some money. I can't remember how much. She said it was just a loan. And she told me that though she hated it, I would have to go because in this small town gossip could kill her and lose her livelihood. She knew some growers from her work and she called a grower and got me a job for the next day.

"I worked a few days but I never went back. Just mailed Kate the money she had given me. And, Ed, I've never talked about this. I've just treasured it in my head. How I wonder how Kate's life has turned out. Maybe someday I'll go back to that town and knock on that door again...."

That reminds me of the one about the one-eyed banker that spent a young fortune buying himself the best glass eye that could be made. It was finished and he went around betting everybody that you couldn't tell which was the glass eye and which was the real eye. He was dealing with a farmer, buying a load of tomatoes, and the banker bet him $100 and laid it down. The farmer looked at the banker for a minute, and pointed out the glass eye. The banker lost. The farmer won. "Tell me — how did you pick the glass eye?" the banker wanted to know. And the farmer remarked, "Well, 'y gad, ye see, I jest went to a lookin' fer the eye that had a little gleam of life an' friendliness fer us farmers in it — the glass one."

Woody Sez, pp. 34-35

A Recall Election and a Free Lunch for Woody

WHEN I WENT TO WORK for the *People's World* in 1938, the offices were in a scruffy building on Sixth Street between Spring and Main. Spring Street in those days was the financial center of the city, banks, and brokerage houses. Main Street, just below us, was and still is skid row. Main Street was filled with unemployed men, migrant workers, and drunks. There were the usual bars, penny arcades, hot dog stands, cheap eateries, flop houses, and employment offices with long lists of nonexistent jobs.

I'm trying to give you some idea of the California scene into which Woody had thrust himself, after years of beating his way around the western states, taking any job he could find and following the crops from one end of California to the other. These were the years when California, particularly the southern part of the state, was going through something very close to a revolution.

In 1934, when the country was in the throes of the Depression and millions were unemployed, there was a writer by the name of Upton Sinclair. He had written a score of muckraking books criticizing what he called the heartlessness, corruption, and brutality of the capitalist system. That year Sinclair decided, or was persuaded, to run for governor of the state.

In the beginning this was a laughable matter. I'm sure that bankers, Hollywood moguls, and heads of industries laughed and joked about it over their cigars and martinis in their clubs and private dining rooms. How could this scribbler, who lived in Pasadena and had no political experience or machine, possibly hope to run for even the office of city clerk? This, in a place where the governor, Frank Merriam, held the state in the palm of his hand and dished out favors to the moneyed people. Where, except for a labor struggle and unrest in San Francisco, business and agriculture were ruled by the open shop, and industry was rampant in its exploitation of workers in the cities and on the growing industrial farms and orchards.

But Sinclair put together a simple, powerful idea under the name of EPIC — End Poverty in California. He asked, "Why not let the unemployed take over the empty factories and the vacant land and produce goods for their own use?" They would not sell these goods on the open market, but would simply produce them for trade and for their own consumption, and thus put an end to waste, poverty, and starvation.

EPIC clubs sprang up all over the state, and the movement grew to a great tidal wave that threatened to inundate California. Sinclair looked like a cinch to be swept into office.

By this time the power clique had become alarmed. In the months before the election, they spent millions on propaganda to turn back the tide. The *Los Angeles Times*, possibly the most conservative open-shop newspaper in the country, poured forth jeremiads about how the Communists were about to take over. Notices appeared in pay envelopes of workers in industry — particularly in the Hollywood industry — telling them that if Sinclair was elected, they were looking at their last paychecks.

Well, Sinclair was defeated by a narrow margin in 1934. But four years later, when Woody was in Los Angeles, the people of the EPIC movement elected Culbert Olson governor in a landslide. Although Olson may not have been the strongest or the greatest governor, by his actions and particularly his appointments, he turned the state topsy turvy.

For example, he appointed Carey McWilliams to head the Department of Immigration, which controlled agriculture and the canneries. McWilliams was a liberal corporation lawyer who later became editor of *The Nation*. He was the author of *Factories in the Field* (1939), a profound sociological study of migrant labor. It was a companion and source book for *Grapes of Wrath*. McWilliams promptly chose Dorothy Healy, who was an organizer for the fledgling cannery workers union, to be his field representative. Her job was to report on the conditions under which migrant farm workers and cannery workers lived and worked.

In that same election, Robert Kenney, an outstanding progressive lawyer, was elected attorney general. He later became a judge.

During the late thirties, an unprecedented reform movement had organized a successful recall of Mayor Frank Shaw of Los Angeles. Shaw headed one of the most corrupt city administrations in the country. Offices were bought and sold, the civil service was a joke, and the infamous police "red squad" ruled the streets, suppressing any kind of free speech or left-wing political organization and cracking down on union organizers.

The whole kit and kaboodle were thrown out of office. Judge Fletcher Bowron, the candidate of a coalition reform movement, became the mayor.

This was a particularly pleasant thing for me and other labor journalists. We could now use the City Hall Press Room, get press cards, attend council meetings, and sit with the rest of the press like respectable journalists.

The key agitator and organizer of this reform movement was Clifford Clifton, a character who could only have blossomed in a nuthouse like Los Angeles. Clifton owned a large cafeteria in downtown Los Angeles, not too far from the *People's World* office.

This cafeteria was a unique place. Kids loved it, for it had a fountain where you could drink soda pop and a belt line with free sherbet. The menu said that you should not pay more for a meal than you thought it was worth, and that you need not pay anything if you didn't have any money. Also, policemen would eat free. I'd always wanted to try out that free gimmick, but never dared.

One day I took Woody over to Clifton's for lunch. He was carrying his guitar; he rarely went anywhere without it. He wandered around gawking at everything, tried the lemonade and sherbet, had a good meal and got his check.

"I'm gonna try this thing out. I'll give it a shot," he said.

So, he went to the cash register, laid down seven cents and said, "It was a good meal, but that's all I got."

The girl at the register stared at him and said, "Just wait on the side a minute."

She called over a young manager who looked like a minister disguised as a civilian. A young, blond fellow with straight hair parted on the side wearing a small bow tie.

"What's the matter, pal, don't you like the food?" he asked Woody.

"Liked it fine," Woody responded, "You can count on me to be a regular customer, Just don't have the do re mi right now."

"Well, how would you like to work in the kitchen for a few hours, or do you want me to call the police?"

"I sure don't care anything about the police," said Woody. "Guess I'll go to the kitchen. As a matter of fact, I'm right handy at that job, having won several prizes for my dishwashing and towel work back in Texas. Yes, sir, I am a seasoned old pearl diver."

I was, of course, perfectly willing to pick up the tab, but Woody waved me off and followed the manager back into the bowels of the restaurant.

I wandered around the neighborhood for about half an hour and then went back to the restaurant, picking my way through the crowded tables, wandering from room to room, stopping at the fountain for a little more free lemonade and watching some kids pick up their free sherbet on the assembly line. I finally located the kitchen, which I found by following a bus boy.

I went through the swinging doors into the kitchen. It was an enormous room and there was a great clatter of activity, with chefs and waiters bustling and shouting orders back and forth. I followed the bus boy past all this clatter, through another door to where the dishwashing was going on. There, above the noise and shouting, beyond the bent heads and steam, I saw Woody, perched on a high chair and singing some of his ballads.

He stopped when he saw me.

"Take a seat, Ed, and make yourself at home. Some of these fellers are friends of mine. They listen to me on the radio. We probably did stoop labor in the same fields and ranches and drank in the same bars all the way from Texas to California. Ain't that right fellows?" Woody said to the big towheaded kid who was busy with pails and suds over at one of the sinks.

"Shore nuf," the kid said, An older man said, "Woody, whenever you want some grub, just slip in the back door over yonder. We've got plenty here."

Photo courtesy of Woody Guthrie Publications Inc. ▲

Lonesome Valley

You've gotta walk that lonesome valley,
You gotta walk it by yourself,
Nobody here can walk it for you,
You gotta walk it by yourself.©

Woody Guthrie Folk Songs, p. 37

Bound for Glory

IT MUST HAVE BEEN LATE 1975, when they were beginning to shoot the movie *Bound for Glory* based on Woody's autobiographical book, that I received a phone call from Harold Leventhal. He had been Woody's agent for many years, and after Woody's death continued to administer his affairs for the family. Leventhal has also been the agent for Pete Seeger, Judy Collins, and Joan Baez. For years he had been trying to put together a story of Woody's life that would work for a movie script. Three different scripts were written over a period of seven years.

"Our trouble," said Leventhal, "was that we were trying to cover too much ground. When we finally decided to center our story on the two or three key years of Woody's development, around 1938, then the whole thing came together and we got a script from Robert Getchell that we felt would work." Leventhal was coproducer of the picture. It was being done by United Artists, who were prepared to spend between five and seven million dollars.

Leventhal had called me because he wanted some help in rounding up material from the *People's World*, and he wanted to discuss some aspects of Woody's activities during the period the picture covered. When he came to see me, I found a short, stout, friendly man, nattily dressed and with a cigar in his mouth. We spent several hours exchanging anecdotes about the Guthrie family and telling each other about our activities in the thirties.

Much of Leventhal's life has been given to working for recognition of Woody's genius and trying, with Marjorie Guthrie, to set up an organization for research into the causes of Huntington's chorea. He also raised money, through the publication of Woody's work and through concerts, to create a fund for Woody's children—all of whom live under the cloud of this disease.

Leventhal invited me to come to Isleton, near Stockton, to watch the making of the first part of the picture. And so I drove out to Stockton. About half of a Holiday Inn there had been taken over by the *Bound for Glory* company. It was a hive of activity. There were a dozen downstairs offices, and many of the cast, staff, and technicians were living in rooms upstairs. I found Leventhal and soon afterward we set out for the location. As we drove through Stockton I remembered the place as I knew it thirty-five years ago, when it was little more than a village. It was now a thriving city with big buildings, a large downtown area, rich residential streets that stretched for miles, grassy lawns, and a whole network of freeways crisscrossing the town. We drove out of Stockton, through miles of cornfields, wheat, alfalfa, and vegetables, thirty miles to the town of Isleton, on one of the many sloughs in the delta.

"It took a long search to find this location," said Leventhal. "We had scouts out for months looking for a place that has remained relatively unchanged during the past forty years. The director is Hal Ashby. He directed *Harold and Maude*, *The Last Detail*, and *Shampoo*. Hal is a stickler for accuracy and detail.

"Now this first location is supposed to be a street in Pampa, Texas, where Woody lived for a while and worked as a sign painter."

We were at the edge of the town now, and Leventhal laughed and pointed to an ancient water tower. On it was painted "Pampa, Texas."

"By the way," said Leventhal, "we sent scouts out to look at the address you gave me in Los Angeles, where you used to live when you knew Woody. And we found the cottage next door that Woody moved into with Mary and the children. The houses are still the same, but there are television aerials on the roofs. Other things on the street have changed. So we found some other houses in east Los Angeles that will work better for us."

They had really found a Depression street here in Isleton, with beat-up, half-abandoned, flea-bitten buildings—old drygoods stores, a few shabby cafes, a little grocery, empty shops—a welfare street. There were about two hundred people in the technical crew, and several hundred actors and townspeople hired as extras were in the street. There were at least one hundred beat-up, old vehicles, some loaded with old furniture, bed springs, mattresses, wash tubs, and pots and pans hanging from the sides.

The people, the extras sitting around and rambling up and down the street in their resurrected thirties clothing, looked as battered and dusty as I remembered them when they filled the roads and the skid rows of Los Angeles. The kids were barefoot, dirty, and ran in packs.

The shooting started in front of the grocery store. Woody, played by David Carradine, had a job to paint a sign. The grocer

A scene from the migrant workers' camp at Isleton, built for the film *Bound for Glory*. ©Copyright 1975, by United Artists.▼

had apparently told him to paint it yellow or black. Woody, with a bunch of kids gaping at him, had painted it red. The grocer comes out, sees Woody's sign, and shouts at him to get out of there and stop his "lolligaggin' aroun'." They shot this little

---

David Carradine as Woody in the film *Bound for Glory.* ©Copyright 1975, by United Artists.▼

scene, two minutes of film about half a dozen times before the director got what he wanted.

I asked Leventhal why he happened to pick Carradine. He granted that it was a hard decision. Arlo Guthrie would have liked to do it, and others were suggested. But Leventhal felt it would be distracting to use Arlo. As for the rest of the actors and extras, he wanted people who were relatively unknown. The extras were all from the town. He wanted an authentic, documentary look.

"There's the head cameraman." Leventhal pointed to a tall, thin, white-headed fellow in a blue jersey. "Haskell Wechsler. He's the fellow who recently did a documentary on the Weathermen that caused a big flurry because he refused to give the government any of the details. He's one of the best cameramen in the industry. Let's move over there and I'll introduce you."

"Ed Robbin?" Haskell looked at me searchingly. "Why, I used to read your columns in the *People's World* every day. That was thirty-five years ago. Actually, I sold the papers on the waterfront in those days."

"Shhh," warned Leventhal.

"I don't care who knows it," said Wechsler, laughing.

Around the middle of the day they broke for lunch. Several hundred people moved to a big lot where the chow wagons had prepared an elaborate feed — rolled cabbage, mashed potatoes, sweet corn, salads, fruits, and all kinds of drinks. Mountains of food for people play-acting a time of struggle and hunger. It took me back to the days in the thirties when ranchers, trying push prices up, sprayed great hills of oranges with gasoline and burned them and poured milk into the ditches of Los Angeles County while children of the Depression refugees went hungry.

The people spread around the lot with their trays or gathered in the dining hall of an abandoned schoolhouse. Leventhal and I took our trays inside, too, and sat down at one of the tables with Robert Blumoff, the coproducer. Blumoff, for thirteen years head of production for United Artists and now an independent producer, must have played a large part in getting United Artists to put up the cash and agree to distribute this movie. Across from me was Guthrie Thomas, the music coordinator. He was talking about David Carradine.

"I can teach him to play and sing in Woody's style, but someone will have to tell him to listen to me."

"Well," said Blumoff, "I don't think Hal wants him to imitate Woody."

"No, I understand," said Guthrie (not related to Woody's family), "But we want to get across something of his style, the nasal twang, the simple way that was part of Woody's delivery."

As we walked back to the street again, people were gathering to resume the shooting of the scene in front of the grocery store. I wondered what Woody would have thought of all this. I decided he probably would have walked off the set and gone to join one of Cesar Chavez's picket lines where workers are still fighting for a decent life.

Dust Storm Disaster

On the fourteenth day of April
Of nineteen thirty five,
There struck the worst of dust storms
That ever filled the sky.

You could see that dust storm coming,
The cloud looked death-like black,
And through our mighty nation
It left a dreadful track.

From Oklahoma City
To the Arizona line,
Dakota and Nebraska
To the lazy Rio Grande.

It fell across our city
Like a curtain of black rolled down,
We thought it was our judgment,
We thought it was our doom.

It covered up our fences,
It covered up our barns,
It covered up our tractors
In this wild and dusty storm.

We loaded up our jalopies
And piled our families in,
We rattled down the highway,
To never come back again©.

Woody Guthrie Folk Songs, p. 102

Mary Guthrie

IN THE LATE FALL OF 1976 I was invited to the preview of *Bound for Glory*, at a theater around the corner from the Beverly Wilshire Hotel. The leading actors, including David Carradine, all of the Guthrie family—both wives and all of Woody's sons and daughters, dozens of people from the press from all over the country and other parts of the world, and hundreds of celebrities and people involved in Woody's life or the production—all these people gathered to see the film and attend the banquet provided by United Artists. Many were quartered at the luxurious Beverly Wilshire at the expense of the film company. It was a gala affair, and an opportunity for me to see the picture and to renew my friendship with the Guthries.

I was particularly interested in seeing and talking to Mary Guthrie, whom I had not seen since 1941, except for a brief meeting on the set at Isleton. My wife Clara was with me. She and Mary embraced warmly when we got together in the lobby on the afternoon before the preview.

Clara and Mary had had a warm relationship when the Guthries lived in the cottage next door to us. Clara had helped set up the house and had given Mary a hand with the children.

We found a private niche where we could talk. I explained to Mary that I was working on this memoir and wanted to get her recollections of the years she spent with Woody.

"You know I'm remarried, Ed, and I have a new life, a very good life with my husband. Of course I've been helping Margie as much as possible with the fight to find solutions for Hunt-ington's chorea. After all, Woody's death didn't end that prob-lem for me, since both of my daughters have come down with the disease. Here's Sue now," she said, as a thin, tall young woman came to join us, walking unsteadily, her body shaking and trembling.

Sue was slender, with brownish blond hair and an open, warm, smiling countenance. This was a great outing for her, and we could see how much she loved meeting people and enjoyed the attention she was getting from everyone. Her face shone with happiness and a child-like joy. I suggested that she and Clara go to the coffee shop while I talked with Mary. What follows is what I remember of that conversation.

When we were alone I said, "Mary, I want to try to get a feeling for what went on in your marriage to Woody . . . what went on underneath. I know it's not easy to talk about."

"Well, Ed, it's a long time ago. In the beginning back in Okemah and then Texas when Woody and I first married, it was a real lark. Woody was a fun person, always on the move and with a thousand things going on in his head. Every day coming around with new ideas and new doings.

"I enjoyed his learning the guitar and tinkering with songs and music and all the strange musician people we met and the dances where he played. The moving around from place to place and Woody doing all kinds of odd jobs — that was an adventure, too, after the small-town sheltered life I had led with my par-ents.

"I didn't mind the being poor and getting along the best we could on the few dollars Woody earned. Everyone else was poor, too, so that didn't matter — not until the kids came. Then it began to be hard.

"We were married in Pampa, Texas in 1933, and it wasn't until early 1937 that Woody moved to California. I went out there to join him later that same year. By then I had two little ones, the two girls, Sue and Gwen.

"You saw the place where we lived in Glendale. It was one room in a broken-down motel. Woody was running all over the countryside, sometimes following the crops and getting a little work, sometimes just hanging around skid row, drinking and playing the guitar.

"There were times when he would disappear for days. Or he would stay home moody and drinking and picking at the guitar or writing his songs.

"I know it wasn't easy for him either, scraping along on whatever few dollars he could pick up at the bars. Then he got on KFVD and started making a little money that people sent to him and feeling good because so many wrote to him and sent him their quarters or their dollars. Guess that's about the time he met you at the station.

"But he'd still go off for days, and I wouldn't see him or know where he was or where the next dollar was going to come from.

"Our son Bill was born in 1939, October, out there in Glendale, and while he was being born Woody disappeared for at least three days.

Mary Guthrie, with Clara and Ed Robbin. ©Copyright 1975, by United Artists.▼

"Somewhere in that time I went back to Texas and then returned to California in 1940. That's when we moved in the house next door to yours.

"You want to know how I felt about all of this? I felt rotten. It was bitter. I was hardly part of his life and that was why I finally decided to get out of it all and I left and went back home.

"It's long ago and I got rid of the anger and bitterness. All the same, these last years it's me that has had the sorrow. Bill getting killed in an auto accident and both girls sick with chorea. The sorrow, too, of Woody's long suffering with the disease.

"So for me it's been wonderful to help in a small way in Margie's work of organizing to support research for a cure.

"Woody was never lazy. He hustled around in Texas when we were first married, getting all kinds of jobs. He could turn his hand to anything, not just music. But he never held on to a job. He got restless and ran off to do something else.

"Many a good job he walked away from, and the same thing held good when he finally began to make it with his music. As soon as he got a chance to make money on the big stations, he couldn't stand it and he'd walk away.

"It's as though he hated the idea of making a lot of money. Never could hold onto a dollar when he had it. Spent it or gave it away. Or drank a good deal of it with the people he met in bars or friends and musicians.

"Don't get me wrong, though. Woody was a good, gentle person—at least when he was sober. He loved children. When we lived next door to you and he was pounding away at his writing, the kids would be crawling around him or under his feet. It never bothered him. He'd take them up and work with one of them on his lap, or stop and sing them a song or tell them a story or just roll around with them on the floor.

"It was hard, though, for me to forget that he disappeared when I was having Billy.

"Such a restless soul. He had to be moving all the time and always getting involved with people. Chasing off with Will Geer to sing around the camps and countryside, or just stopping at Will's house for days without telling me or worrying about me and the kids. Well, I learned to accept that but I couldn't see any future for us in all this. That's why I picked up and went back home.

Two postcards from Woody, who was in the army, stationed in Illinois, in 1945.

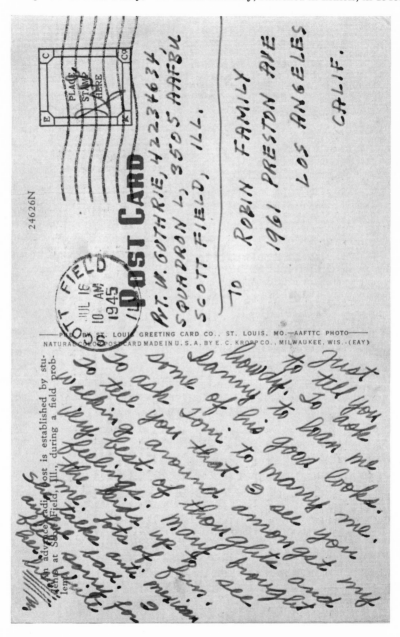

its Four Thirty for our
first morning roll call
and Five Twenty for your
School call. The clouds
look like rain and the air
is cool but half the sky
is clear. The boys argue
in the barracks about
who swept and mopped and
who didn't. They are half
asleep and gripe about any
old thing. They smile to
talk about the atom bomb
and wish you could invent
one big one just to touch
off all the people that
start these lonesome
wars. I wonder why some-
body doesn't invent of
bomb that you can
drop and it will throw
up a block of nice
new houses? You could
figure it out, Danny.
How are all of you? Write.
I like your letters.
woody

"And somehow I managed to raise the kids, working, getting occasional money from Woody and help from my folks. And after all that my son grows to twenty and then gets killed and the two girls are both stricken. Well, Ed, that's life, the good and bad. I've no regrets and things are a lot better for me now."

As Mary and I talked in our little niche, we could see the crowded lobby with its glittering chandeliers and exciting hubbub. Photographers were moving about with their gear, and newsmen were buttonholing some of the celebrities. An air of excitement and suspense was building up for the evening performance.

And there we were, Mary and I, trying to resurrect the anxieties and feelings of thirty years past. I could see that Mary, though she had been involved to some extent and been helped by the success of Woody's records, books, and songs since his death, was still astounded by the fame he had achieved. The man she had known had played the guitar and picked out songs like many others where she grew up.

She must have asked herself many times — what was so different about Woody and why was he being accorded this kind of attention? How difficult for her to understand that the man who may have been neglectful and irresponsible with his own family was able to touch such deep and lasting chords in multitudes all over the world, because in his songs was a passionate love and concern for the poor and the tormented.

Love casts out hate,
Love gets rid of all fears,
Love washes all clean,
Love forgives all debts,
Love forgets all mistakes.[©]

Born to Win, p. 167

La Peña

ONE NIGHT A FRIEND called to tell me about a gig of Woody's songs and stories at a Berkeley spot, La Peña.

La Peña is a restaurant, a gathering place for sympathizers of Chilean and other South American revolutionaries. It has a hall where there are nightly performances — music, poetry, lectures, dramatic spectacles usually representing the labor or revolutionary scene. Woody would have liked La Peña. And he would have liked the place next door, too — the Starry Plough, a similar gathering place for Irish revolutionary sympathizers.

On that night in the fall of 1977, Lenny Anderson was singing a selection of Woody's songs, accompanied by a good guitar. Between songs, Bruce Greene read, eloquently, some pieces selected from Woody's books. Forty or fifty young people were there, some with children who wandered around or sat close to the platform and listened with rapt attention.

Anderson's rendering of the ballads was simple and straightforward, an easy folk style reminiscent of Woody's singing. While he tuned his guitar between songs or brushed his long, red moustache, he told of the origins and the times of the songs. Greene followed with readings from *Bound for Glory*, *Woody Sez*, and *Born to Win*, telling of Woody's early life in Okemah and Texas, of his hoboing days or his philosophy of life and what he had learned in the course of his wanderings.

One song particularly touched me and made me think of the talk I had had with Mary, an interview that I had written up that very day. The song, called a "Hobo's Lullaby," was written by Goebel Reeves, who died in 1959. Woody used to sing it often.

Go to sleep my little hobo,
Let the towns drift slowly by,
Can't you hear the steel rails humming,
That's a hobo lullaby.

Do not think about tomorrow,
Let tomorrow come and go,
Tonight you've got a nice, warm boxcar,
Safe from all this wind and snow.

I know the police cause you trouble,
They cause trouble everywhere,
But when you die and go to heaven,
You'll find no policeman there. ©

It so well expresses Woody's tenderness for the down-and-outer, the lost and wasted people he met on the freight trains and in the hobo jungles. And yet, the same man was able to cause Mary bitterness and sorrow feelings of loss and desertion.

In the intermission, I introduced myself to Anderson and he asked me to tell about my friendship with Woody. I got on the platform and told my story. I was warmly received.

After that performance, Lenny and Bruce asked me to join them in future shows. We named our show "An Evening with Woody Guthrie," and we began to get more and more calls. We did interviews and parts of our show on radio station KPFA. We performed just about every month at La Peña, then at the Julian Theatre in San Francisco, and at Fort Mason, a wonderful cultural center that has been created from an old army complex in north San Francisco.

Somewhere along the line we picked up Art Peterson, who joined our group with his gentle and humorous rendering of Woody's children's songs. Then we began to get gigs in the surrounding towns, Sebastopol at a large pizza parlor, Mendocino, Fresno, and at a ranch in the Sierras. The Fresno performance had a special significance for me. It took place at a small farm on the outskirts of Fresno. The six-and-a-half acre farm is owned by some members of an organization called National Land for People. This group is waging a struggle for the small farmers and for the division of the San Joaquin Valley into small farms.

This valley was supposed to have been divided into 160-acre farms to be homesteaded by small farmers and farmworkers. The government spent millions putting in canals to serve the valley. Then, gradually, the big industrial farmers used tricks to gain control of much of the land. Their tricks included manipulating the distribution of the water rights. National Land has set up an organization to fight these industrial monopolies and also to show how a small farm can be successfully operated.

For our show they had created an open-air theater on one of

Left to right: Art Peterson, Ed Robbin, Lenny Anderson, and Bruce Greene — doing their Woody Guthrie show all over Northern California. ▼

their fields. An old farm wagon served as our stage and bales of hay were set out in a semicircle as seating for the audience. Our theater was surrounded with a high pile of mulched manure that gave a special flavor to the whole performance. About two hundred young people gathered with their children to hear us.

As we sang and told our story, there seemed a special significance to the occasion, as though we were somehow bridging the years between the thirties and the present. Throughout the valley the farm workers were again in the midst of a struggle for a living wage. Of course, the fighting now is different from the Salinas strike that I had witnessed. Now they have a strong union and a dedicated leader in Cesar Chavez. But Woody's songs and the stories rolling over these fields have a special meaning to these people.

Who are the people in this performing group of ours? Until recently, Lenny Anderson worked as a pressman in a print shop. He decided he would try to make a living doing what he loves best, his music. Lenny graduated from the University of Chicago and did graduate work at Stanford. He majored in History, then decided the academic life was not for him. Lenny spent about a year in South America, traveling with his friend Jenny Stamm. He played his guitar and Jenny sang, and they made their way through the Americas performing. Lenny learned Spanish and picked up many Spanish folk songs.

Bruce Greene, who speaks pieces from Woody's writings between the songs, grew up in Los Angeles and graduated from UCLA where he, too, majored in history. Bruce is a high-school teacher. He does oral histories and teaches the techniques of doing such recordings. And he plays the harmonica, too.

Art Peterson, who came from San Diego, earns his living working at a San Francisco sewage plant. Art has spent a number of years teaching in child-care centers and is well known in folk music circles on both sides of the bay.

Our show has grown and become a smooth, professional performance. We have become friends, sensitive to one another on and off the stage.

Out there in Fresno the morning after the concert, Lenny stood in a stubbled field and called to us.

"Hey, you guys. I got something to say." We gathered around him. "I want you to know how good it feels to do this thing together. It's become important to me and I know it is to each of you. I guess what I'm trying to say is that I love you and feel good with you. That's all. I felt I had to say it."

Each of us mumbled some kind of embarrassed acquiescence as we stood in the sun.

Woody and Will

AS I LOOK BACK to the day I brought Woody over to Topanga Canyon near the Santa Monica coast to meet Will, I ask myself how it was that there was such immediate contact between these men, contact that became a long and deep friendship. That friendship lasted through Woody's life and long after, because Geer made a second career of singing and talking about and promoting the life and legend of Guthrie.

Now I can see that the two were very much alike in many ways. Take politics. Neither was a political theorist. Neither bothered about what was the correct line to follow. Both Guthrie and Geer had always known which side they were on. Woody often sang the song, written by the wife of a Harlan County, Kentucky, miner, with the refrain, "Which side are you on, Which side are you on?" But that never was a problem for him. He and Geer both had always been on the side of working people, of the poor and the oppressed. They both had a passionate need to search for a way to a better world.

For many years Will was blacklisted, both in Hollywood and on the Broadway stage, because he lived out that need. Even when he was at the height of his success in movies and television, he traveled the country, speaking for any progressive candidate who needed help in his campaign.

And both had a creative need to bring their talents to people everywhere, to entertain and teach and plead for an end to war and exploitation. Together they traveled the country, to towns

Will Geer when he was long, lanky, and Lincolnesque.

and villages, union halls, money-raising gatherings, to homes and halls, singing, playing, acting, and always trying to get people to organize on their own behalf.

When I first wrote this chapter, it was mostly about the friendship that grew between Will Geer and Woody Guthrie. I had just been working over the introduction to this chapter and recalling how I brought Woody to meet Will in 1939, when I heard that Will had died in Los Angeles.

On the evening of the Sunday when I heard of Will's death, I was scheduled to be part of a program on Woody Guthrie at La Peña, a Berkeley cabaret frequented mainly by Chilean and other South American supporters of guerilla and revolutionary movements of the Latin countries. This was a program that Lennie Anderson, Bruce Greene, and I had done many times. Usually Lennie sang Woody's songs, Bruce read from Woody's writings, and I told of my friendship with Woody and of the political and social background of the thirties that shaped his songs and his writings.

However, that night I dwelt on my long friendship, and Woody's, with Will. I realized as I spoke that Will's passion for his gardening was closely related to his relationship with people, particularly young people. For just as he planted and nurtured growing things wherever he was, Will was always surrounded with young people whom he helped, loved, and involved in both theater and politics.

Will Geer, known and loved by so many people as the grandfather in the TV show, "The Waltons," was part of the fabric of the American theater.

Years ago he played Jeeter in *Tobacco Road* on Broadway. He was a Shakespearean actor and spent a long period on the east coast with the Stratford Theater. He had been a political radical since the early thirties and was one of the first to feel the heavy hand of the blacklist, in Hollywood and on Broadway.

At the time I got to know Woody, Will was living in a canyon in Santa Monica. He got occasional movie work. But he spent much of his time doing political skits or with his own group of people, singing madrigals and Elizabethan songs in colleges or at parties. Mostly, however, he was busy developing his garden.

For his great love, next to the theater, was gardening. He had graduated from the University of Chicago in horticulture and ever after, whenever he had the chance, his fingers were in the earth planting, pulling weeds, and cultivating whatever little patch of ground he occupied. He became an expert on the plants and flowers referred to in Shakespeare. When I went to see him play "Coriolanus" at Stratford in Connecticut, he took me to look at the Shakespeare garden he had developed.

Sometime in the thirties, when he was with some company in Chicago and I was living in the close-by city of Gary, Indiana, he came to visit and stayed a couple of days with us. Early in the morning after his arrival I peeked in the attic, where he was supposed to be asleep, and found the bed was empty. I stepped out to the porch and looked out over the big, straggly, neglected yard with some fruit trees, lots of weeds, and wild flowers. And there was Will, in his shorts, digging around the trees so they could be properly irrigated.

"Ed, you're a disgrace to the human race, letting this garden go like this. These trees tell me they haven't had a drink for weeks. You could have a fine vegetable patch and some real good flowers. Shame on you."

"Clara is the gardener, not me. We haven't been in this

Will Geer and Clara Robbin in Berkeley in the late 1960's.▼

house that long, but she'll get to it. She loves flowers. The only thing I can raise is radishes. I'm really good with radishes."

In the afternoon Will said he wanted me to take him to the adjoining town of Hammond, Indiana, to see a nursery he said was famous for its development of all kinds of herbs. At that time I was in the house-remodeling business and had an office right there in Hammond, but I had never heard of this plant nursery.

We drove out and for a couple of hours Will talked to the robust owner and picked seeds for his Shakespeare garden. I learned later that that nursery was famous among gardeners all over the country.

I speak of this because I think there is a key to the kind of person Will was in his love of trees and plants. Through all the years I knew him, he loved and nurtured not only things of the soil but also people, particularly young people.

I'm sure that dozens of youngsters got their start in the theater through the various theater groups he put together in different parts of the country. Wherever Will lived, wherever he stopped, there were theatricals and performances and young people clustered around him to work with him.

When he was blacklisted on Broadway, he started a coffee cabaret on the east side of New York. I believe that was in the late forties. It was called Folksay. Anyone with any talent for singing, dancing, or acting could perform there. I remember that my daughter Tamara, who was attending dancing school at Julliard, danced there one evening.

I met Will in 1926 through my friend Meyer Levin, the novelist. That was fifty years ago. Meyer and Will had just graduated from the University of Chicago and invited me to travel with them to Europe. We hitchhiked from Chicago to New York and then to Montreal. Hitchhikers were not as common then as they are now, nor were there as many cars on the road. So we spent many a day walking. And as we walked, tall, lanky Will, with a stick in hand, pointed to trees and plants and named them for us. And he stopped to talk to farmers and discuss the crops, while Meyer gloomily trudged on ahead of us, impatient with our dawdling.

When we got a ride, Will was always the one to sit with the driver, and before long whoever was driving the car would be on close terms with him. One fellow who picked us up was coming from his fiancee's funeral. Soon, with tears running down his cheeks, he was telling Will all about his troubles. Will nodded and softly consoled him. The fellow was on his way to Washington, D. C., and that was quite a jump for us. We had been sleeping out in the fields at night. The first night that man insisted that if we were going to sleep out, he would, too. The poor fellow got very little sleep because the ground was hard and the mist was heavy. The next night he begged us to take a room in a hotel and he would pay for it. When we got to Washington, there was an emotional parting from Will, and we had to promise that man we would look him up on our way back.

Eventually we got to Montreal and down to the docks there. After a few days we signed on to a cattle boat for Liverpool. The day we arrived in Montreal we decided to celebrate by stopping at a fancy tea and pastry shop. It was all so foreign and English and exciting, as though we were already on the continent.

The menu said tea and pastry for a set price of a shilling. The friendly, blond waitress brought us a large pot of tea and then set a platter of lovely French pastry on the table. We looked at each other in some amazement. All this for a shilling a piece? So we ate the whole platter of pastry. When the bill came we were flabbergasted to find that we owed several pounds, quite a dent in our meager finances. We acted, though, as if we were quite aware of what we were doing, paid the bill and then laughed it off somewhat ruefully when we were outside.

The work on the cattle boat was rough, particularly for a tenderfoot like me who had never done any heavy work. You'd carry full buckets of water down to the cattle stalls, two buckets at a time through the long passageways, and then the damned cows would knock the buckets over in their eagerness to drink. During that trip Will often found ways to help me with my end of the work when he saw me wearing out.

Since that adventurous trip, Will's path and mine have crossed many times. We met at the Goodman Theater in Chicago, soon after I got back from Europe. I was a student actor, and one day while sitting in the green room studying my lines, I saw an elegant gentleman come in with spats, a cane, and a monocle around his neck. I looked real hard. Sure enough, it was Will Geer. He'd come to see about directing a play. And a couple of years later he did direct a play for the Goodman.

Sometime in the middle thirties I was asked to direct a play at a settlement house. The cast was mostly black working people from South Los Angeles. The play was *Stevedore*, written by Paul Peters and George Sklar and had been very successful in New York with Rex Ingraham playing the leading role. The play was about longshoremen on the New York waterfront. I needed a white sheriff and asked Will to do the part. Although he was an old pro and I was not, he never hesitated, attended all rehearsals, and never interfered with my direction.

I still remember one incident on opening night. The first scene is played in a tiny beat-up waterfront coffee house. The sheriff comes in to roust some of the lads around who are sitting on the stools. One of the lads had hidden himself behind the counter because he figured the sheriff was looking for him. After the sheriff leaves, the fellow who was hiding had a cue he failed to pick up. But the man who played the lead wandered back of the counter and found him fast asleep. He had to shake him awake. The fellow had worked hard all day and simply fell asleep back of the counter.

The play was a big success. These working men were amazingly good actors, although none — except for Will and Clarence Muse, who played a preacher — had ever been on stage before.

In 1976 I was doing an article about Woody and the making of the film *Bound for Glory*. I thought it might be useful to talk to Will so I called him in Los Angeles and asked if he could spare me some time.

Will said, "I'm having a birthday party in a couple of weeks. It's my seventy-fifth birthday and some people want to celebrate. So why don't you come down for the party and then afterwards we can talk."

So a couple of weeks later I piled Clara into the car and we beat our way down to Los Angeles. It turned out that the little birthday party was at the Santa Monica Civic Auditorium, which was packed with thousands of people and hundreds were turned away. Will was using the occasion to stage a folk song and drama festival to raise money for a Woody Guthrie fund. The money would be used to find a cure for Huntington's chorea, the disease that killed Woody.

There were streamers all over the auditorium congratulating Will, and he sat in center of the stage rambling and directing the proceedings in an easy, informal way. But the whole performance centered on Woody. It was a loosely-knit program that included Pete Seeger, Arlo Guthrie, Will's number one wife (he always referred to her that way) Herta Geer, his daughters Ellen and Katie, and his son Thad. There were other singers and actors. The performance included dozens of Woody's songs and anecdotes, and I was surprised when Will told about how I had brought Woody to see him not too long after I met him at KFVD.

The meeting was a great success. The wildly enthusiastic audience was made up mostly of young people, lots of girls with their hair loose over their shoulders, men with beards and moustaches and young children running up and down the aisles or sitting close to the stages.

The next day I went to Will's house. He lived in one of those Spanish cottages in a courtyard. He had the rear cottage and apparently owned and and rented five or six other flats. A big sign at the gateway read, "No actors allowed on thses premises," which I took to be a joke because the young people I saw lounging around the courtyard were obviously reading or studying lines and others, who wandered in and out of the living room while Will and I talked, came to take up various problems they were having with the agents or studios.

On the way to Will's cottage, I had noticed that the courtyard was thick with plants, flowers and trees, all carefully nurtured, and I remembered again that plants and trees had been the love of his life and that he had been trained as a horticulturist.

Will, when I met him some five decades ago, was a tall, slender, Lincolnesque figure. He had now grown considerably in bulk and had a flowing mane of gray hair. He wore flowing garments and sat like a great, calm Buddha, waving people in and out of the crowded little living room which was cluttered with comfortable old furniture that looked as if the pieces were early vintage Good Will and Salvation Army. On the walls were pictures of Will in some of the many movie and theater productions he had been in—pictures with Katherine Hepburn, Katherine Cornell, Claude Rains and dozens of other movie

Will Geer at a rehearsal in Topanga Canyon. ▶

greats. There were pictures of the scenes with the people in the "The Waltons" of whom Will spoke as though they were really his own family. Will was a warm, affectionate man who genuinely loved people and surrounded himself with them.

Will sat on the couch next to me and I taped our talk. Here is the transcription of that conversation:

Robbin: You must be worn out after that great shindig last night.

Geer: No, no. I've had a fine rest and I'm ready to go. You want to talk some more about Woody? You brought him out to the canyon and Herta and Woody got together and played duets and sang together right away. Herta said, "What a marvelous man — too bad he can't sing." You remember Woody had a kind of monotonous way of singing. All those wonderful words and sometimes he sang them so poorly. You really had to listen to the words to appreciate him.

Robbin: You really took him under your wing, didn't you?

Geer: Well, Woody felt at home with us. I took him up to the studio and introduced him to David Ward Griffith and to Louie Milestone, but I could tell they were thinking what's Will doing with that hillbilly singer. I was testing along with Burl Ives for the part of Slim in *Of Mice and Men* because I'd been in the play on Broadway — you know that Steinbeck thing. I met Steinbeck there at the studio.

Robbin: I guess you met Stenibeck later, too, didn't you?

Geer: Yes, quite a bit later, don't remember just when, but after Woody's songs had begun to be sung around, I introduced Woody to Steinbeck and he said, "Took me years to do *Grapes of Wrath* and that little squirt tells the whole story in just a few stanzas." We all had a good laugh over that.

Robbin: He was talking about *The Ballad of Tom Joad*.

Geer: At that time we were making that film *Fight for Life*, and I got Woody into that picture, I suppose because his wife Mary was pregnant — fragrant, he always said — and I played the doctor. And Herta was pregnant, too, and my daugher Katie was the one who was born during that picture. At that time, too, I met two young boys sunning themselves somewhere out on Eagle Rock and they turned out to be Cisco and Slim Houston. You remember how close Woody and Cisco became. Cisco was a fine musician. He and Woody worked together a lot and later shipped out together and were torpedoed several times in the same ships. Slim lost his life when one of his ships sank.

Anyway, while this picture was being made as a side thing on a very short budget, we'd get together every weekend. John Steinbeck and Paul de Kruif supervised and directed. John lived just a couple of blocks away, at the Garden of Allah Apartments. I remember walking over to John's with Woody one time. We picked up John and we walked right up to the drugstore just about a block away. John stopped on the corner and picked up a copy of the *People's World* at the newstand and a copy of Hearst's *Examiner*. Glen Gordon, one of the actors in the picture, had joined us. He said, "How in the hell can you read that paper knowing the things you know?" And Steinbeck said, "Well, a writer has to know all sides of a question. I have to know what that old buzzard Hearst is thinking and writing." And Woody was impressed with that. It really made a great impression on him, about learning everything.

So later on in New York when I'd take him to whorehouses, he'd say, "Well, Walt Whitman used to go to whorehouses to study." And he'd say, "John Steinbeck said you gotta study all sides of a thing." Woody was a great student and lover of Will Rogers, who came from his own home state. Like Rogers, Woody took his columns right from what he read in the daily papers. Woody saw a song in every headline. And he practically wrote a song every day. Just as in those days, my hobby has been and I guess it always was to learn a poem every day.

Robbin: And what did you see in Woody in those early days?

Geer: I saw this wonderful combination of a fellow who wrote his own poem every day and sang it every day. And I said to myself, what a sorry fish I am. All I do is take words from someone else and say them over and over again. Here was a guy who was creating, even though his things seemed kind of monotonous to me in those days — a lot of people felt they were. He wrote songs about the Ladies Auxiliary of the Union or about L.A. traffic jams, or about the Lincoln Street jail. And now I can see that all these songs touched the lives of the people he was singing to and each had a germ of an idea. He was talking about changing things, making them better. And there was so much sly humor in a lot of his songs. He came over to our house often during that period, when Mary was pregnant and we were all waiting for the picture to start. That was the first real money he ever made—in this picture.

He'd come over to the house and frequently we wouldn't be there. He'd go into the icebox and help himself to something. And in return payment, he'd scrawl a song on an old grocery bag. And we couldn't wait to find out what tune to sing it to. Too bad I've lost songs Woody just tossed off. None of us knew his songs would last the way they have. I think one thing we missed in the beginning about Woody was not seeing that he was a genuine radical. Since Woody loved Will Rogers and tried to emulate him so much, I guess at first we saw him as a kind of Will Rogers. He didn't seem interested in politics—just in people.

Robbin: People were his politics. His radicalism consisted in the fact that he always knew which side he was on. In his songs and in his talk you could see that he always knew who the enemy was—the bankers, the big-moneyed people, the men who ran the munitions factories and helped make wars. It was that simple—like in the western movies where the enemy almost always was the banker and the big railroad tycoon against the small rancher or farmer.

Geer: Yes, and in his outlaw songs the outlaw is a kind of Robin Hood, a good guy compared with the banker who robbed the poor, not with gun but with a pen.

Robbin: As you say, the songs, the way he wrote the songs. Anywhere—on any scrap of paper, picking them out on the guitar as he wrote. He'd be sitting in the back yard, picking on the guitar and then all of a sudden he'd begin singing a brand new song.

Geer: The interesting thing to me about one time like that—speaking about this facility—we had a contest up there at my place in Topanga Canyon. This was a good deal later on, after the war and all. He already showed signs of that Huntington's chorea and his mind was a little wobbly and his pen was scratchy. He was even having trouble with the guitar. We set this up one day, this contest, I mean, and I was emcee. I don't remember who all was there—but Peter Seeger and Vern Partlow, a newspaper man and songwriter, and a lot of other singers and writers and, of course, an audience from around the neighborhood. And I said, "Let's see who can sing the best love ballad." Everyone else sang fairly well-known ballads. But

God Blessed America
~~This Land Was made Forifor me~~   178
                                                        h

This land is your land, this land is my land
From ~~the~~ California to the ~~States~~ New York Island,
From the Redwood Forest, to the Gulf stream waters,
    God blessed America for me.

As I went walking that ribbon of highway
And saw above me that endless skyway,
And saw below me the golden valley, I said:
    ~~God blessed America for me.~~

I roamed and rambled, and followed my footsteps
To the sparkling sands of her diamond deserts,
And all around me, a voice was sounding:
    ~~God blessed America for me~~

Was a big high wall there that tried to stop me
A sign was painted said: Private Property.
But on the back side it didn't say nothing —
    ~~God blessed America for me.~~

When the sun come shining, then I was strolling
In wheat fields waving, and dust clouds rolling;
The voice was chanting as the fog was lifting:
    ~~God blessed America for me.~~

One bright sunny morning in the shadow of the steeple
By the Relief office I saw my people —
As they stood hungry, I stood there wondering if
    ~~God blessed America for me.~~

                * All you can write is
                  what you see.

                        Woody G—
original copy   N.Y., N.Y., N.Y.
of this song   Feb. 23, 1940
                         43rd st + 6th Ave,
                         Hanover House

when Woody's turn came he wrote a new one right there and sang it right off. I wish I could remember it because it was a good song and I don't believe he ever recorded it.

Robbin: When did you first notice his sickness — this Huntington's chorea that killed him?

Geer: Well, it began first in New York. I didn't notice it much until then. When he got to town he came to live with us on 7th Street. He asked me, so I told him we were paying $250 a month for this apartment. At first he thought it was $250 for the rest of the year. He was so upset when he found out that he went down to the Bowery to sleep around and said he wanted to find out the difference between the rich and the poor. At that time I was working in *Tobacco Road* playing Jeeter, so I could afford a place like that. Anyway, I remember I started taking Woody to bookings. I think the first time was something being given by the League Against War and Fascism, somewhere out in

Woody with Joe Louis and Earl Robinson, his friend and the composer of *Ballad for Americans.* ▼

Queens among the aristocrats. It was a big fancy house and he didn't like the setup too much, but we were getting ten or twenty dollars for the night. We didn't have a drink although they had a big punch bowl there. And as he got up to sing, he started to jerk like this. Sometimes you've seen drunks with that kind of jerk. So the hostess accused me of bringing him drunk. I said, "Woody, you haven't been drinking at all, have you?" And he said, "No, no I haven't been drinking." He had this twitch and she thought it was a drunken thing. Actually, I thought he was acting like some of the Bowery drunks as a kind of joke because he didn't like the swells. But then, over and over again, he was doing it more.

Robbin: Was there pain attached to the disease?

Geer: There didn't seem to be any, but he would feel confused as though he were taking something. He once described to me — we had tried smoking marijuana together and he said you think two or three things at the same time. He said "I sometimes get the same feeling as with the drug when the sickness comes on me. I think several things at the same time." The same thing happened to me. Once my kids slipped some marijuana in brownie cookies. I ate a couple of these brownies on this trip back in the car when we were coming from a performance, and I thought I was going out of my mind with my head spinning off all these strange mingled thoughts. Then the kids laughed and told me what they had done. And then I remembered that that was exactly how Woody had spoken about feeling when he was first beginning to feel the disease.

Robbin: I was wondering whether — it had occurred to me, the last I saw of him in California when he had come back from New York for a second time — he was drinking very heavily.

Geer: After he had the chorea.

Robbin: Well, I didn't know that he had Huntington's chorea or that anything else was wrong with him. He always drank a good deal at parties, but he was in control. I believe this was the time when he was traveling with the Almanac Singers. There was a big party at our house and Woody came over with Pete Seeger and a couple of other people. Maybe Cisco Houston was with him. He drank everything in sight. He got very angry with me — the only time he'd ever gotten angry with me — because I ran out of liquor and I didn't want to see him drink any more. He said, "Ed, get some more liquor,' and I said, "No, I'm not going to get any more liquor, Woody, not tonight." He got so angry he just left the party. And I wondered when I heard about the illness, whether....

Geer: The liquor diverted his mind from it. I remembered he brought Cisco Houston to a party in Topanga Canyon — it was after the second World War. You remember Cisco and Woody and Cisco's brother Slim were all in the merchant marine together and had two ships shot from under them. Slim was down in the engine room and Cisco and Woody were topside and Slim never got out. But Cisco, who was very close to his brother, never believed he was dead, figured he had somehow gotten out and been picked up by some other ship. So he kept searching for him. So he had this peculiar obsession and Woody talked to me about it and said we've got to make Cisco realize that his brother is dead. Well, this went on for about a year, with Cisco searching the ships for some sign of his brother. In the spring of the following year, we were all in New York. I was up planting dogwood trees at my place in the country, and I remember it was the day Irwin Cobb died. Woody was with me. I was working in *Tobacco Road* at the time and someone had given me a jug of white lightening. So I went to the woods and Cisco and Woody came along and helped me dig up a couple of dogwood trees. And Woody and I talked it over and decided to dedicate these trees, one to Irwin Cobb and the other to Slim Houston. So we got back to the house and planted one tree and dedicated it to Cobb, this wonderful fellow who'd gone from our midst. And we were all drinking from the jug and we poured a little on the tree we'd planted and then we took the other tree to the other side of the house and planted it and took another swig from the jug all the way around, and I made a short speech dedicating this tree to Slim Houston who was killed in the engine room of such and such a ship — the ship Woody and Cisco were on. Well, the next thing I knew I was out like a light. Cisco hit me right on the jaw and I was out. I woke up with Woody bathing my head and Cisco was just sitting on a log looking mad and drinking out of the jug. Woody took the jug and poured some down my throat and then bathed my head with this damned liquor. And pretty soon we began to sing songs and I can remember the girls coming out of the house — that time they were about four and five years old, and they saw my lying on the ground and they ran in the house yelling—"Mama, Papa's dead out in the yard and they're burying him." So the women all came running out and by that ime we were all so drunk they had to carry us into the house.

Woody with Mary Guthrie and Burl Ives in 1939. Courtesy Marjorie Guthrie.▼

Robbin: Did you ever make the rounds with him, to the bars and skid row?

Geer: Yes, lots of times. Where he liked to go with me a lot was up where the Queen Mary and all those ships docked. There were a couple, three bars there where the French sailors would come in. This was in New York. He'd come up to see me after the show, *Tobacco Road*. He must have see that show forty times. And he'd come up and pick me up after the last act, and we'd walk over about three or four blocks down to the docks, and there'd be one bar where nothing but the British sailors hung out, another bar where the French sailors were, all during the war years, back and forth, you know. And he liked to drink with me there. I never saw him seriously drunk except on one occasion, like I said, and also at a party or two, which was when he was jerking at the same time and it made a peculiar sort of thing, you know. At that time none of us realized what it was. In fact, Woody himself turned himself in. He saw he was beginning to jerk like his mother.

Robbin: There was a period when he stayed with you in Topanga.

Geer: That was later on. He came down saying he had chorea. He'd just come back from a hospital, and they told him about it; and he decided to take another trip West, and he came out and stayed with us for a time. He lived there at the house in Topanga Canyon for about almost a year, in that little shack there. Woody stayed long enough, he got interested in a piece of land down the road from us. It was mostly straight up, called Pretty Polly Canyon. An old fellow down there sold him a piece of land. We were going to homestead it. In the first place, the fire department threw him off because he was always building fires to cook himself coffee and things, and he couldn't do that. So he came back to the shack and stayed with us, and a little later he was going to develop it. In fact, he was still paying on it when he ran off from our place with a girl.

Robbin: She was the wife of this friend of yours, wasn't she?

Geer: Yes, she was the wife of the man I'd taken off to do *Salt of the Earth* with — Marshall, his name was. He played one of the deputies and I'd driven out with him.

Robbin: You were building a house? Was it on Woody's land you were building a house?

Geer: Yeah.

Robbin: You building a house for Woody at that time?

Geer: Yeah, it was out of sod.

Robbin: He was sick. I remember you telling the story that he was sick, sitting on the hillside, singing songs.

Geer: She fell in love with him. Off she marched, off she went with him. Of course I moved this fellow Marshall into my house, I was so sorry for him. Here was my best friend running off with his wife, and I gave him the lead in the show. And we'd been playing for about six months. I was blacklisted so I couldn't play at the colleges and universities, they wouldn't let me go. So I cast him opposite Herta. And old Mary Virginia Farmer one day says, "You notice what I notice, Will?" And I said, "What?"

"Well, they're playing those love scenes real!" And they really were.

Robbin: This was *Salt of the Earth*?

Geer: Oh, no, these were just bookings we went out on, our folklore and bookings. We'd come back from *Salt of the Earth* with this fellow, Marshall, and while we were away doing the picture Woody had absconded with his wife. And Mary Virginia says, "That's just too bohemian. I thought you were just good solid working-class people. That's just too bohemian."

The summer about a year later he came to visit us in New York. He was living with Anya then, the girl he'd run off with, Marshall's wife, and Woody and Anya had had this baby, a little girl. I was living in this house in the village which we had converted into a Folksay cabaret because I was still blacklisted and couldn't get any work.

Robbin: Why were you blacklisted, Will?

Geer: Well, that was the time when we were doing everything we could in the anti-fascist and anti-Nazi fight—singing and talking and trying every way we could to show people the meaning of Naziism—and so a lot of writers and actors were being blacklisted. That was a long time before McCarthyism, which came after the war. Anyway, Woody would lay the baby on the kitchen table and it would be yelling and screaming there while he wrote skits for us to do or new songs, and Anya—I think that was her name—would be trying to quiet the baby. But her crying didn't seem to bother Woody. He'd just keep right on writing. Anyway, I should mention that the baby was adopted out because Anya didn't want to keep her. And that girl grew up and then ran away from her adopted parents—she took dope and lord knows what else, and she was finally killed in an auto accident. I only heard about that recently, when the family that had raised her wrote me about it.

Robbin: How old was she?

Geer: Oh, she was eighteen or nineteen years old and was killed in an auto accident about a year ago.

Robbin: I don't think I've ever known anyone who was so pursued by tragedy, disease, fire, and death.

Geer: Yes, that's true. Reminds me of Edgar Allen Poe with his child-bride and his constant failure in life—his addiction to drugs and alcohol. Arlo Guthrie, Woody's son, makes more money on one recording that Woody did in his entire life.

Robbin: But what was so extraordinary was that in spite of all the terrible things that happened to him and his family, his attitude was always so up. Look at his pictures and you'll see that he even held his head up high.

Geer: No matter what happened in the world or to him personally, he faced it cheerfully and confidently and tried to put it into a song that would make people think and feel.

Robbin: When he lived next door he'd sit out in the back yard with the kids, watching them play and picking out songs. I think that was when he started those children's songs. To my mind he created a new kind of children's song. They are all as though he was able to get inside children and see the world through their eyes—like

> *Why, oh why, oh why*
> *Because, because, because, because*
> *A hammer's a hard head*
> *Why can't a dish break a hammer*
> *Why, oh why, oh why*
> *Goodbye, goodbye, goodbye*

And then half a dozen verses that follow that are full of a child's questions and fantasies.

Geer: Or that song—"Put Your Finger on Your Nose, on Your Nose". I've seen kids singing and doing that song all over the country. I think he must have written several hundred songs for children. Remember—"Wrap yourself in paper and mail yourself to me"—and that marvelous patriotic children's song—"My daddy flies a plane ship in the sky."

Robbin: Can you think of any of the other bookings you went out to?

Geer: Well, there were so many—but, yes, I remember one of the first ones in New York was in a rich house up at Steven's Landing. Actually it was at Katherine Cornell's house, you know, the actress. She was a friend of mine and there were a whole group of people assembled on New Year's Eve. And I said,

"Woody, we can make some dough here. They asked for a ballad singer and I said we'd come over. They wanted somebody like Burl Ives, but he wasn't available, so I told them I had a fine new ballad singer." I had told Katherine that Woody's fee would be $50. So I took him along to this party with all this fancy food and bar and everything under the sun. All the women were dressed formal. I remember Woody noticed they were all shaved under the armpits and that made a big impression on him. And the men had on white shirt fronts—dressed to kill. Well, I got Woody there to sing and he was just impossible. He kept his eyes shut while he was singing and looked away from the people and just kind of yawled his outlaw songs. I went up to him and said, "Woody, sing your dust bowl ballads. This is a social-minded group. And why do you keep your eyes closed?" Woody said, "Their white shirts dazzle me. Get me outa here, Will." It's the same kind of thing that made him walk out of a job at Radio City when they called him a hillbilly singer. Money never meant anything to Woody.

Robbin: Along that line, I remember I read an account by Alan Lomax—who admired Woody greatly and did several hours of interviewing Woody for the Library of Congress—of how Woody walked out on a big radio contract during his first trip to New York. Apparently the Target Tobacco Company had signed him up for a series in which he would be backed up by an orchestra of fifty musicians. Woody lasted just a few performances. That was all he could take. It was just too rich for his blood. He took that money he made and bought a brand new car and started back to Oklahoma.

Geer: I remember that very well.

Robbin: According to Lomax, he got rid of the car in Oklahoma City. But I know different. He picked up his wife Mary and the kids and drove the car back to Los Angeles to my house.

Geer: Yes, Woody loved a fast car and he would drive it like hell on wheels, and he loved women and they loved him and clustered around him like bees around a honey pot. I frequently quote that passage out of his book *Born to Win*—some of it goes like this—"I was torpedoed two times in the merchant marines during the war and I figure that whatever guilty feelings I owed to the race I paid off by these two torpedoes, and I paid off some more by laying out eight in the army with a uniform on. So, my woman came to me so strong and so plain while I was at sea and in the camps that I swore and vowed that I was going to have to find love at its fullest and highest in order to make up for the wet dreams in my ship and army bunk. Every other man felt this same way. Several hundred thousand that I spoke to felt this same way. I went about with naked visions of naked, naked, naked you in front of my eyes for so many months that I vowed and swore that I would eat you up from your head down to your toes if you would so freely allow me to do it. I smelled your skin and your hairs just as plain, plainer, those days and nights on those troopships and in those army cots. I made you such a thing of glory in my mind that I wanted to lick you down like a big pile of dark brown sugar.

"If there is a prettier sight on earth than those patched hairs between your legs, I've never seen or heard about it. If there's a

Will Geer with Ramblin' Jack Elliot. Photograph by David Gahr.▼

prettier sight than this long and viney root that stands up here between my legs, I've certainly never seen that. My pecker hard, my pecker soft and limber, my balls, my sack and my bag, my crotch, my legs, my root, my rod, this climbing long and jumping pole, this thing that is my gate of life, this door of mine through which we flow, this chord, this rope, this prong that I pass my finest creation through, I pass my own self through, I pass you down and out and in and through, this planting tool, this hose, this dong, dick, this stick and rod and staff of birth."

Robbin: There's a big difference between the Woody who wrote that poetic passage and some of the other poems and prose in *Born to Win* and the Woody I knew in those early days in Los Angeles.

Geer: Yes, some of the folk quality, the naiveté is gone.

Robbin: I've tried to trace that—I think what happened was—sailors do a lot of reading and Woody spent a couple of years in the maritime service. Between getting torpedoed he evidently read a good many books. Then, after the war, those years in New York with his wife Margie were years of cultural growth. In one of his pieces he speaks of Sandburg, Whitman, and Pushkin. A whole new world of literature and theater opened up for him in New York.

Geer: Yes. Years before, when he made the records for the Library of Congress, Woody said that the two greatest men who ever lived were Jesus Christ and Will Rogers. That sounds kind of simple, but Woody really loved Will Rogers and hoped to emulate him.

But to get back to Woody's erotic or sensual writing—I know he was acquainted with Whitman way back, because I caught him reading a copy of Walt's *Leaves of Grass* right in my house and we had a long talk about Whitman. And I think his song "So long it's been good to know you," which is sung everywhere now, comes right out of Whitman. Woody was very impressed with the fact that my number one wife Herta and I were married to the verses of Walt Whitman all those years ago. Herta was the granddaughter of Mother Bloor, the grand old lady labor fighter and organizer and one of the founders of the American Communist party. Woody loved the sensuality in Whitman. He had the same wide, democratic feeling for his fellow men—liked to move among them, live and touch all their lives. Like Whitman, he loved to catalog the names of places as well as the bodies of men and women and all their parts.

Robbin: Yes, he fingered people and places and names of places like a professional card dealer lovingly riffles a deck of cards. In his sensuality he reminds me of D. H. Lawrence. That's why I feel he must have read him. The sexual lyricism in the piece you quoted a bit ago....

Geer: Oh, he was full of that. People used to say that was part of his disease. That's nonsense. Like most poets, Woody was deeply, passionately sexual in his life and in his work. That reminds me—because I used to use those quotations in my folklore shows that I did traveling around the colleges. In fact five or six years ago, at the University of Michigan, students said when I quoted that piece—you know I was doing a thing mainly on Whitman and I quoted that piece and they said, "Where is that in Walt Whitman? I've never read that in Walt Whitman." And I'd say, "That was Woodrow Wilson Guthrie." "Well," they'd say, "it sounds just like Whitman."

Robbin: Will, you had that period in New York, I guess it must have been in the early fifties—when you were blacklisted and you were doing a lot of the folksay type of things in the Village on the weekends.

Geer: Yes. Woody was living with me on Bank Street at Auntie Mame's and about that time he took to writing plays for us. We kept having to move from one place to another because the fire department or the city would kick us out. We played on the east side and on the west side. Harold Leventhal was one of our first managers. [Leventhal, in addition to being an agent for Woody, Pete Seeger, and Judy Collins through the years, was coproducer of "Bound for Glory".] Harold was a young clothing manufacturer then. Rex Ingram and Fred Helliman and lots of other actor friends joined us to put on these plays. We'd collect money and then split the take because we were all unemployed. I remember Woody had just come back from the south, just knocking around and playing and singing, and he fell into a fire and hurt his hand. Somehow the Guthries were always getting burned in fires. He made a little violin while he was laid up. And he left that violin at Auntie Mame's. Woody liked to sleep in the basement on a window ledge. He liked the air and he liked to watch and hear the people in the street. There were some drunks living upstairs on the third floor, and one day they threw some water down just as Woody was sticking his head out the window, and he got soaked.

Robbin: You were saying something about the plays he was writing.

Geer: Yes, he started to write these crazy plays with casts of hundreds. He had a whole German Army Corps in one and it was about some sisters who had a hotel that became a whorehouse. It was in a Soviet city occupied by the Germans. The sisters would invite the German soldiers in one at a time and when the soldier would get excited the sister would cut his dong off and shove him through a collapsible bed into the basement to bleed to death. And when they finally got to the general who was too old to get an erection, they had to poison him. The show ended with a new regiment marching in. The sisters got all worn out with cutting off and dropping penises through the floor.

Well, that was in the beginning when he was just feeling his way into playwriting. But he wrote many plays about strikes and the labor movement, and some we did. I had a pile of them and they all disappeared or were stolen. I think it was about this time the chorea was sneaking up on him and his writing began to get wild and uncoordinated. And then soon he was in and out of hospitals as the disease progressed.

Robbin: Sometime in the late fifties I came to New York and visited the Folksay performance. There was Woody backstage. He was pretty sick by then and shaking all over. Apparently they'd let him out of the hospital for awhile. He took me to a cold water flat where he was living and he showed me a thick manuscript he was working on. It must have been about a thousand pages. I thought it was a sequel to *Bound for Glory*, His wife Margie told me recently that she has someone going through that and editing it. [This became the book *Seeds of Man* — a raucous, Rabelaisian account of a trip to Mexico to hunt for gold.]

Geer: Yes, we had a place out in the country and Woody used to come out there and write on that book.

Robbin: You said something about his having been in a fire. Was he burned in a fire?

Geer: Well, Woody and Anya went down south somewhere — first to Florida and then to some town in Georgia where there was some struggle Woody wanted to be part of. And they were camping out along the way and Woody had one of his spells of sickness and got to shaking so bad he fell into the camp fire and his arm was burned so bad he couldn't play his guitar. He seldom played after that.

Robbin: Fire just pursued that Guthrie family. Wasn't it his daughter Cathy who died in a fire?

Geer: Poor thing. Yes, that was later. He was living with Margie in New York, down in the Village. The little girl was only four years old, and how Woody loved that child. He wrote many of his children's songs at that time. They were for Cathy. No one really knows how it happened. The child was left alone for just a few minutes and a fire started, caught her clothes, and she died in the hospital.

Robbin: I remember reading Woody's story about it. He told it as though he had to get it out of his system, the whole story in every small detail with all the agony of the child's death in the hospital. She lived a few days after the burning. Fire pursued the family from way back. In Okemah his father built a big house, and before they had hardly moved in, the house burned to the ground. Later his mother was burned, and his sister Claire died of burning from a coal fire. It's just incredible.

Geer: The Guthries were pursued by tragedy. The boy William, the one who was born in the movie we made, *Fight for Life*, that boy died in an auto accident when he was twenty years old. And Mary's two daughters have both been stricken with Huntington's chorea. One is already hospitalized. [That daughter, Gwen, has since died.]

[I turned off the tape recorder and suggested to Will that we go out for some lunch. We drove over to the Farmers' Market on Fairfax. On the way Will recalled early days with Woody. Back in the early forties, soon after Will met Woody, they used to sing and play together at street corners or meetings, or out at the camps of migrant workers and at lots of parties for different causes. But at that time neither of them was making any money. So they would get paid a small fee and take the rest out in eating—things like knishes or chopped liver and gefilte fish at the Jewish gatherings. Will figured that's where he learned about Jewish cooking.

We wandered among the lush produce stands of the Farmers' Market and stopped for a special compound of fruit and vegetable juices that Will insisted we drink—a mixture of coconut, parsley, and pineapple—and then sat down with salad and a sandwich.

But it was hard to talk, because young people kept surrounding Will to get his autograph or to ask him about some member of the famous Walton family. I had forgotten how well known he is as the grandfather in the Walton show on television. Young actors came to whisper in his ear or ask for favors. And Will took it all quietly and seriously, greeting everyone warmly.

When we got back to the house, I asked Will about Arlo Guthrie and his relationship with Woody.]

Geer: In the beginning Arlo didn't want to ride on his father's coattails, so he rarely mentioned and even avoided singing his songs. But then after his big success with that motorcycle song and the movie *Alice's Restaurant* and all that, he was free to sing Woody's songs.

Robbin: Arlo has his own kind of humor. He's got his own thing.

Geer: His real concern, though he tries not to talk about it, is the disease—Huntington's chorea. He's just about the age when it hits. But Arlo just decided to live as though that thing didn't hang over his head. So he married and has a couple of kids and bought a ranch out there in New York State and is busy fixing up a big old house between concert tours.

Robbin: Woody had four children with Margie.... Isn't that right?

Geer: Yes, Cathy, who we talked about and who died by fire—then Arlo, and a girl Nora, who's a very fine modern dancer in New York City, and Joady, who lives in San Francisco and teaches guitar there. Woody named him Joady after Steinbeck's character Tom Joad.

Robbin: Some months ago we were invited to Joady's wedding. He was marrying a lovely blonde woman named Aileen, with whom he had been living for several years. I mention that because this seems to have become the new pattern for young people around our area. They live together and then after a time, if the relationship survives, they get married.

Geer: Not a bad pattern . . .

Robbin: They were married in a charming, vine-covered Lutheran church on the south side of San Francisco. It was all very traditional. Margie was there with her new husband, and Arlo dressed in an elegant white suit with a lacey shirt, and Nora, whom I hadn't met before, and her dance partner. The small church was filled with friends of Joady's and Aileen's— almost all young people in their late twenties or early thirties.

Will and I had spent the whole day together. It was almost evening and the room was darkening. Will was wrapped in his Mexican blanket. His head had dropped and I think he was beginning to doze off. Time to leave. I sat opposite him, just staring and remembering all the years we had known each other, all the times our paths had crossed. Did I, perhaps, have a premonition that this was the last time we were to meet?

Soon I waked Will from his sleep.

"Will," I said, "you should write it all down. Tell the story of your life, if only for your grandchildren and your friends."

"I'm going to do it, I really will."

We embraced warmly.

"Come back soon. Lots more to talk about," Will said as I left.

COMMENTS ON WILL GEER

There was a lilt to his voice and it made you want to listen. . . . He liked people who sang songs that meant something to him.

Arlo Guthrie

I never saw him downhearted in all the years, not even in the "frightened 50's." When I think of Will, I think of vigor; there was never any energy crisis for Will Geer.

Pete Seeger

You never expected him to die, but to go on and on and on. What I remember about Will is the word "roots," I always associated him with earth — there was earth in the way he walked and earth in the way he talked.

Morris Carnovsky

He's the only man I know that knows the vegetables by their maiden names. When he shouts, the vegetables come a-running and jump in the stewpot.

Woody Guthrie

My father built a theater which is alive and well and which is where his spirit lives.

Thad Geer

With or without Will in front of us, we know he's with us, right?

Marjorie Guthrie

New York Times
Sunday, May 14, 1978

I'm a dust bowl refugee,
Just a dust bowl refugee.
From the dust bowl to the peach bowl,
Now that peach fuzz is a-killin' me.

We are ramblers so they say,
We are only here today.
Then we travel with the seasons,
We're the dust bowl refugees.©

Woody Guthrie Folk Songs, p. 74

Marjorie Guthrie

I HAVE MET Marjorie Guthrie, Woody's second wife, on and off through the years since Woody's death. We saw each other in New York, on her occasional visits to San Francisco, and on the exciting weekend when the movie *Bound for Glory* was previewed. This is an approximation of our conversations at various times.

"You want to know how I happened to meet Woody and what it was like living with him?

"Well, I think it happened about 1942. I was living in Philadelphia with my husband but frequently came to New York, where I studied with Martha Graham and also taught dancing.

"Once I came to New York with a friend and we stopped for awhile at the old Almanac House on Tenth Street in the Village. She wanted me to meet some of the people there who were her friends.

"As I remember we were in a large loft-like room in this ramshackle building, and no one was around except for a curly-headed fellow off by himself in a corner picking on a guitar.

"That was Woody. We met and talked briefly. I was immediately taken with him and used to drop in from time to time to listen to rehearsals.

"The group was having a hard time getting Woody to keep the beat. He'd wander off in his playing, I suppose because for so

long he had been used to playing to his own beat or leading anyone he played with. Also, he never played a song the same way twice.

"So I would work with him on this since, as a dancer, the beat was like a metronome in my blood. We began to see each other and walk through the city together. We became lovers and Woody couldn't stand it when I went back to Philadelphia.

"He would write me letters daily that were volumes — passionate, crazy letters — urging me to leave my husband and come live with him. He would write letters to my husband, too, that it was wrong of him to keep me when I loved someone else and that only he, Woody, could fulfill me as a woman, an artist, and a lover. It was a heady, painful time.

"But then, eventually, it all came to a head. I came to New York to live with Woody, got my divorce, and we were married.

"Our life was crazy, intense up and down. I was dancing and teaching. Woody wrote and worked with the Almanacs. He loved to be with people, with friends. He loved to roam around the city and to stop in bars to drink, to play his guitar, to talk and to listen. Sometimes he would write all night and in the morning I'd find him asleep in the table. After coffee he'd read me what he had written. Writing to him was as natural as breathing.

"We had Cathy and I had to spend more time at home. Those were the war years and Woody was in the merchant marines. There was the fear, the agony of waiting while he was away, particularly after his ship was torpedoed. This happened twice. Well, I learned to live with it and we would have wild times between voyages.

"Later — I guess it was sometime after the war and after Woody had spent time in the army — we took a place on Coney Island not too far from the beach.

"It was there that our little Cathy burned to death in that cruel, accidental fire. I can't tell you what Cathy had been to us, and how wonderful a companion she was to Woody. He used to stay home and work while I went to teach my class. Woody would play songs for her while she drew pictures for him. Many of his children's songs were written in that period.

◀ Left to right: Joady, Woody, Margie, Nora, and Arlo. By this time Woody's illness is quite advanced. Photo by David Gahr.

"It seems to me that it was after Cathy's death that I began to be aware of Woody's sickness. He drank more than ever and occasionally went into wild rages. Sometimes he disappeared for days. I got used to it. I knew he'd be back. Meantime the other children were being born—Arlo, Nora, and finally Joady."

I asked Margie whether Woody was aware of his importance as a songwriter and author.

"I can only say that he had a tremendous feeling about himself. It's as though he felt he had a mission. He'd say, 'We're poor now, but one day our kids will be rich.' We made a joke of it and talked about what the kids would do with all the money that would be coming in. And then he would say that his one hope was that the kids would be aware of the need to change the world they lived in and become part of the struggle."

Woody with Jean Ritchie, around 1946. Courtesy Marjorie Guthrie.▼

"Where do you think his politics came from, his passion for helping the underdog?"

"In the first place, you have to realize that his father was politically involved in Okemah. He held a city job. Also, he wrote a book saying that socialism couldn't work in the United States. He was a man who was self-educated, read widely, and studied law on his own. In his book on socialism, he quotes people like Bernard Shaw, and not many people in those days living in Okemah were reading Shaw. Woody loved his father, but even as a boy he didn't agree with him. The family argued about politics a lot.

"Basically, though, Woody's strong feelings came from his experience of the Depression in Texas, working at all kinds of jobs, meeting people. Then the overwhelming catastrophe of the dust storms, his life as a migrant worker, knocking around the country on freight trains, rubbing shoulders with the unemployed and the families that were dispossessed by the banks.

"A greater awareness of the organized struggle came from his getting to know people like you, Ed, then Will Geer, and later Pete Seeger.

"I'm frequently asked whether Woody was a Communist. Woody learned to believe in a world of sharing. He constantly talked of organizing and unions, but he would never have been able to fit into the Communist party and follow a political line. When he was asked, I remember he used to quip, 'Some people say I'm a Communist. That ain't necessarily so, but it is true that I've always been in the red.'"

Once I asked Marjorie how she felt about Woody's straying off with other women and his irresponsibility toward his earlier family.

"When Woody would get upset, he would leave me. I knew he would come back because I knew he loved me and the children. I knew I was living with an unusual man, a man of genius, and that you pay for that kind of experience. I think I learned as a young woman that Woody created an image of frailty, of needing to be cared for, that women responded to. He touched their motherly instincts. Women wanted to mother him.

"Then, too, I learned and understood when Woody would go away that he wasn't running away from me. He was going to do something or to experience something and that is not running away.

"Woody was a loving man. Maybe his greatest and most permanent love was for his men friends, for people like you and Will Geer, who helped open up a new world of understanding for him. Then his great friendship with Cisco Houston and Pete Seeger, who were part of his musical crusade, and Alan Lomax, one of the first to understand and appreciate his songs. Woody's feeling for his songs and his destiny were deep and passionate, and this superseded everything else."

Since Woody's death, this frail-looking little woman, who decided that her life would be devoted to combating the disease that killed Woody, has built a nationwide organization to fight Huntington's chorea.

It is a difficult, uphill struggle. But when I was in New York last year, I sat in her office and heard her talking to congressmen and senators and watched her fly off to Washington to testify before congressional committees. She and her organization have become a force in the struggle for research and for health programs for this country.

*If ever I die, don' bury me
On Wall Street under a cement tree,
Where folks can look at the marble slab
And all this trash and obstructory.*

*But if I die and when I do,
Just cart me out where the sky is blue,
And have some carrier carve this peice,
Woody knows just where he is.*

Woody Sez, p. 167

*When death has closed my eyelids,
And my race on earth is run,
Will you miss me when I'm gone?*

*Will you miss me, will you miss me,
Will you miss me when I'm gone?*

*Come sit yourself beside me,
Come sit beside my bed.
Lay your hand upon my brow
While my aching heart grows dim.*

*Will you miss me, will you miss me,
Will you miss me when I'm gone?*

Born to Win, p. 232

Huntington's Chorea

THE DISEASE, Huntington's chorea, has twisted itself through the whole Guthrie saga. It sent Woody's mother to an insane asylum and eventually killed her. It gave Woody fifteen years of debilitating torment and finally killed him. It struck both of Mary's daughters and killed the younger, Gwen. And it still hangs, a threatening cloud, over the lives of Marjorie's children.

And there may be more. It seems possible that the fires that so tragically pursued the family were also related to the disease. Fire destroyed the beautiful home built by Woody's father, caused the death of his sister Clara, and the terrible and strange death of his daughter Cathy in New York City.

In *Abnormal Psychology**, Huntington's chorea is described as follows:

> This degenerative disorder was first described by the American neurologist George Huntington in 1872, after his father and grandfather, both physicians, had observed the disease in several generations of a family. Symptoms usually begin when the individual is in the thirties and thereafter deterioration is progressive. The early behaviorial signs are slovenliness, disregard for social convention, violent outbursts, depression, irritability, poor memory, euphoria, poor judgment, delusions, suicidal ideas and at-

---

*Davison and Neale, p. 420.

tempts, and hallucinations. The term chorea was applied to the disorder because of the patient's choreiform movements—involuntary, spasmodic twitching and jerking of the limbs, trunk, and head. These signs of neurological disturbance do not appear until well after behavior has already started to deteriorate. Facial grimaces, a smacking of the lips and tongue, and explosive, often obscene speech are other symptoms. The afflicted individual is likely to have severe problems in speaking and walking. Eventually, there is a total loss of bodily control. Death is inevitable, but it may be delayed for ten to twenty years after the onset of the illness.

The following excerpts from the biography* of the American folk singer Woody Guthrie illustrate the development of the disorder, some of the prominent clinical symptoms, and the personal tragedy of the illness.

Describing the first signs, Woody's wife, Marjorie, commented:

> *"What confused me, and Woody himself, in the early stage of the illness, was that by nature he was a rather moody person. As early as 1948 we began to notice that he was more reflective, and often depressed by trivial things.... [Shortly thereafter] the symptoms of the disease became more obvious. Woody developed a peculiar lopsided walk and his speech became explosive. He would take a deep sigh before breathing out the words. The moods and depression became more exaggerated and more frequent.*

In 1952 the first serious attack occurred. As his wife described it,

> *"Woody had a violent outburst and foamed at the mouth."*

He was hospitalized for three weeks and diagnosed as an alcoholic. After his release he had another violent seizure which, this time, led to a three-month hospitalization.

Later, Marjorie said,

> *"The disease was making rapid progress. Woody found it increasingly difficult to control his movements, appearing to be drunk even when he*

---

*Yurchenco, pp. 139-148.

> *wasn't drinking. Friends watched with apprehension*
> *as he dived into traffic, oblivious to danger, Chaplin-*
> *like, warding off each car as it sped toward him."*

Finally, in 1956, it was recognized that Guthrie had Huntington's chorea, and he spent his remaining years in hospitals. One especially poignant incident which occurred
shortly after his hospitalization, is related by his wife:*

> *"In the early years of his stay in hospitals, Woody*
> *would leave every now and then on his own. One day*
> *he took the wrong bus and landed in some town in New*
> *Jersey. Noticing his dishelved appearance, his dis-*
> *traught air and halting gait, a policeman picked him*
> *up, took hom to the local police station, and booked*
> *him on a vagrancy charge.*
>
> *Woody told the police that he was not a homeless bum*
> *but a sick man. He explained he was staying at a New*
> *York hospital and begged them to get him home.*
> *"Well," they said, "if you're sick you can stay in our*
> *hospital." Finally, they let him call Marjorie and she*
> *went tearing out to New Jersey.*
>
> *When she arrived she was received by a staff doctor, a*
> *Viennese psychiatrist. "Your husband is a very dis-*
> *turbed man," he said imperiously, "with many hal-*
> *lucinations. He says that he has written a thousand*
> *songs."*
>
> *"It is true," I said.*
>
> *"He also says he has written a book."*
>
> *"That's also true."*
>
> *"He says that a record company has put out nine rec-*
> *ords of his songs." The doctor's voice dripped disbelief.*
>
> *"That's also the truth," I said.*

The disorder is a genetically determined one, passed on by a
single dominant gene. The offspring of an individual with
the disorder have a 50 percent chance of being afflicted. A
postmortem examination of the brain of an individual with
Huntington's chorea reveals widespread atrophy and scar-

---

*Yurchenco, 1970.

ring, The major pathological change is a loss of neurons in the caudet nucleus, one of the basal ganglia. The cerebral cortex also atrophies, especially the frontal areas. High levels of dopamine in the caudate nucleus appear to be primarily responsible for the choreiform movements.

I Ain't Got No Home

I ain't got no home,
I'm just a ramblin' around,
A hard workin', ramblin' man,
I go from town to town.
The police make it hard wherever I may go,
And I ain't got no home in this world anymore.

Now as I look around,
It's mighty plain to see,
This wide, wicked world is a funny place to be,
The gamblin' man is rich and the workin' man is
poor,
And I ain't got no home in this world anymore.©

Woody Guthrie Folk Songs, p. 35

Woody's Death

WHEN WOODY DIED on October 3, 1967, the *People's World* asked me to write something about Woody for the paper. This is what I wrote:

Woody Guthrie is dead.

He was fifteen years dying, torn by an incurable muscular disease that made it impossible for him to play the guitar and make the songs and the music that bubbled and surged in him all through his life. In his autobiography, Woody said he made his first song when he was two years old.

> *Listen to the music*
> *Music music*
> *Listen to the music*
> *Music band.*

And through the fifteen years of slow dying, echoes of the growing recognition of the genius who had written a thousand songs must have come to the sanitarium in New York. Many of the songs are part of the language, are sung by thousands who do not know his name—will be sung as folk songs are for generations to come.

Recently Joady Guthrie, Woody's youngest son who lives in San Francisco, teaches guitar, and has begun to write his own songs, came to our house with his wife Aileen and spent the day with us.

Of all the children, Joady looks and acts most like Woody. He is medium height, slight, and has dark, curly hair. I took him aside, asked to hear some of his songs, and said I'd like to talk to him about his father.

One of Joady's songs was a sad, crying blues, black inspired. Here are the words.

> *Sweet magic woman,*
> *She moves like a mama snake.*
> *Sweet magic woman,*
> *She moves like a mama snake.*
> *She's got so many curves*
> *Don't know how she keeps from*
> *Makin' no mistakes.*

> *Blind man walkin',*
> *He can feel her passin' by.*
> *Blind man walkin',*
> *He can feel her passin' by.*
> *She's so good at passin'*
> *He says: "My, my, my!"*

> *When she goes down to the river,*
> *She wades up to her thighs.*
> *When she goes down to the river,*
> *She wades up to her thighs.*
> *Lord, I just can't keep from lookin',*
> *And I just can't apologize.*©

We talked of Woody, whom he had only known in illness. He talked slowly and with hesitance, remembering times when Woody was out of the hospital for a weekend visit and the family was living in Coney Island.

"He would take me to the fields or the beach and we would sit for a long time looking for insects or shells and Woody would talk to me about these things."

I asked Joady what he felt about Huntington's chorea, since he is approaching the critical age when there is a 50 percent chance of it striking him. At first he said he'd rather not talk about it. But then after a silence he said:

"I suppose what I feel is fear. But I'm philosophical. Everybody dies sometime, and if I have to go that way, so be it."

"In the first place," I said, "fifty percent, that's not bad odds. And second, largely due to your mother's effort, there's a reasonable chance those odds will improve."

I had then intended to question him about how he remembered his father. But I was extremely touched when Joady said, "It would be very important to me to know how you saw my father. What I mean is, all I heard through my life was that he

Arlo, Joady, Nora, Marjorie, and Stewart Udall, receiving the Department of Interior award for Woody. Photo courtesy of Marjorie Guthrie. ▼

was a great man and a genius. He always had a halo on his head. So in a sense I was deprived of a father, a real living person. You know what I mean? I really want to know what kind of an everyday man he was."

"Well, Joady, he was a simple, fun-loving man. He liked to be with people and sing songs to them. He was a man who loved the world and all that was in it, and yet he knew things weren't right and he wanted to help change things.

"He was full of passion and he loved women, many women. You know from his songs how deeply he cared for children, his own and other people's children. He was full of humor about his own and other people's troubles.

Woody, with Harold Levanthal (rear), son Arlo (center), and Marjorie Guthrie in 1966, receiving the United States Department of Interior's Conservation Service Award in recognition of his life-long efforts to make the American people "aware of their heritage and the land." Photo courtesy of Marjorie Guthrie.▼

"Were you there when he died?" I asked.

"I visited him shortly before he died. He was trying to pick at the strings of his guitar. He enjoyed that even with his shaky hands. But I particularly remember his saying, 'Well, Joady, chorea is doing me in, but then Korea almost did the country in.' So you see he had his little joke even at the end."

"What was the funeral like?"

"He was cremated and they put his ashes in an urn. Then only the family went out to sea in a small ship. It was a cold, autumn day. The sea was choppy and we all stood around while they scattered his ashes on the water."

Nobody need weep for Woody. His memory lives and he was always truly Bound for Glory.

Legend

HERE IS AN ILLUSTRATION of how Woody's story grows as time goes on. *The Home Front*, a Time-Life book by Ronald Bailey, tells about the time in 1942 when the hysteria against Japanese-Americans was at its peak, just before they were herded into concentration camps in one of the shameful episodes of our history.

It seems that Woody and Cisco Houston were in a skid row bar in Los Angeles, drinking beer and playing for nickles and dimes. There was a crash of glass next door and when Woody and Cisco went out, they saw an ugly crowd of people who had just broken the window of a saloon owned by a Japanese couple. The crowd was shouting obscenities and threatening violence. Woody and Cisco pushed their way between the crowd and the Japanese couple and started to play and sing union songs, including "We will fight together, we shall not be moved." Soon the crowd quieted down and gradually shuffled away. By the time the police arrived, the problem had disappeared.

A Letter from Woody

I DREAMED OF WOODY. I don't dream often. At least I don't usually remember my dreams. But this time it was as clear as if it was really happening. Woody came to me as if he was just arriving from far away. He was young as he was when I first met him, and he seemed impatient to get on with something.

In my dream I said, "Woody, you've come just in time. I'm going on the air in a little while to talk about folk music, so I'll just say a few things and then you can go on and play your songs."

"Let's go," he said.

He wasn't carrying his guitar, and that struck me as unusual because Woody almost always carried his guitar.

On the way to the studio he kept saying, "Why don't you get on with it?" I thought he was talking about my driving, because I do tend to dawdle, particularly when I am driving with someone. Later I realized he meant I should get on with this book and finish it.

When we got to the studio, people surrounded us in wonder and someone said, "What are you doing here, Woody? You're dead."

"What of it," said Woody. "Jesus rose, why shouldn't I?"

My dream gets vague after that.

I guess the reason for my dream was that in rummaging through some papers recently I came across a long letter from Woody. He had dropped us cards or letters every so often but back in those days we moved often and things were lost or left behind. Besides, I never was much of a hand at filing or saving things.

However, a few things have survived over the years—a postcard from the time when Woody was in the army, the long letter below (the last page of which I am unable to find), and, possibly most moving to me, a Christmas drawing and message on a folded piece of paper towel. On the front is a drawing in pink paint, possibly of a dog, signed "Cathy." This must have been sent shortly before Cathy burned to death. On the back, signed "Guthries, Woody, Marjorie, Cathy," is a message typed, I am sure, by Woody:

> *You are the closest family of people I know or owe.*
> *I owe you a lot more than a holiday card*
> *but think that will be settled later.*
> *Cathy makes good cards, don't you think so, Tony?*
> *[Refers to my daughter Tamara.]*
> *We exploited her child labor and worked*
> *her 49 hours per day to get a card for every one*
> *of our friends.*
> *There's a little piece about Cathy in this*
> *January issue of the kids magazine, 2 to 8.*
> *Danny can run and scout out one.*
> *How's L.A.? All union yet?*

On the inside of the toweling is scrawled in blue paint, LOVE, and then again the three names.

What a tragic loss this child's terrible death must have been to Margie and Woody. Woody wrote most of his children's songs for Cathy. He wrote of how he worked and played with Cathy at his side, and of her death, in his book, *Born to Win*.

And now, here is the letter I unearthed the other day. Woody never dated his communications but I would judge this letter was written in 1941 at Almanac House.

> Howdy Ed, Clara, Danny and Tommy:
> How's all of the broke down toilets around your neighborhood by this time, also all the stinking politics? Also all the big chess players? That sounds like the name of a vaudeville troupe.

Being along with the Almanac Singers is some sort of a treat to me, as it is poking my head full of this stuff called Organization. Something that I still need a heap more of. But it's the only way to do anything. We got a good organization going, and it seems like each feller knows which cylinder he is expected to fire. Lee Hays, the boy from Commonwealth, is a real student, and has got several years of theater work and song-leading back of him. He knows a lot about vigilantes down south, and is a pretty fair talker along with it. Peter Seeger, maybe I told you about him before, he's the big, long, tall boy from upper New York State. His dad is an expert when it comes to music and folklore, and Pete's better than his dad. Pete writes our notes down in good shape and swears that it's possible to just look at them and play a tune. This is a new experience to me, as I always played by ear, and couldn't tell you the difference between a sheet of music and a bunch of turkey tracks. Mill is our organizer, commissioner of writing letters, getting bookings, and keeping dates straight. a hell of an important thing they tell me, and as I write, I'm damn near inclined to think so, too.

We're coming head on with most of the young theater groups across the country, and they're teaching us a lot of things. But in Chicago they got one of the best, it's called the Chicago Repertory Theater, kind of like TAC, but better got together. We had some long talks around other people's tables, and learned that not all show folks agree all the time. We been thinking it was our religious duty to work out a criticism of the theater groups in general, and to tear into Eli Steigmeister, and take a few pokes at Blitzstein, because we just naturally ain't satisfied with a lot of things they do, Steigmeister's song book, the *Treasury of American Song* (parts of which seem to of been snuck out of the new and unpublished manuscripts of Alan Lomax's coming book, *This Singing Country*, plus a couple of borryd off of me without the rattle of any coins). Our mainest criticism of a cross section of the show groups would be that we can't help from thinking that they are going to the wrong end of the line for their material, and that they are copying a hell of a lot from the nickel machines, Hollywood, Tin Pan Alley and the rest. We ain't got nothing against the higher forms that a music note can take on, but there's one big thing that these folks has got to remember, and that is that their work leaves a good impression, and tells the right political tale, and that it leaves something with the people that hear it. The only way for a show man to make dam shore that he's giving the people something they'll like and *remember*, is to make goddam certain and shore that it comes from the people in the first place. I don't know how to talk to these really brilliant actors and actresses that are so young, peppy, smart, and anxious to learn. But we stumble into talks and debates, and sometimes some mighty good misunderstandings.

We say it's the people, and we say the most important thing we got to do is to beat everybody that's like Hitler, and we say the biggest and just fight in this direction is the Union fight—and the job of the organized to organize the ones that ain't . . . . and it might not sound like bragging, but that's really what I aim to do when I pat The Almanacs on the back and say, By God, fellers, do you know that *we've* sung for more numbers of people than most any other bunch I know of, and while whole big bunches of actors that are twice and a dozen times as talented as us have beat their heads against the floor, and hollered, Goddam, goddam, folks, we got good stuff, but how the hell are we gonna approach the Unions? *Approach*, hell. You don't approach the Union. You just haul off and walk-in.

Naturally, in this new set up with the Almanac Singers, I expect to run onto whole herds of college graduates, geniuses, female geniuses, and highly intellectual guys, but I ain't a gonna hold back a damn bit from saying what I think at the time that I'm thinking it. You might spew off a whole slew of wild ideas and words that schools don't teach, and maybe one out of every hundred there'll be a couple of good ones. Well, from what I've seen and heard of the works of folks like Mister Steigmeister, just about two good healthy words of any kind would cause his whole organization to run down to the hock shop and buy guitars, and tune up, and run down and go to singing in saloons, and keeping an eye peeled for material.

I'm pretty well satisfied as long as my family's a getting along in decent shape, but you know that being separated from them or broke or bent, might cause me to take an extra snort when I oughtn't to, and this kind of stuff might not have made a polished talker out of me, but there's one thing that I do know, and am proud to say, and that is this thing that they refer to in the Archives of Americana as folklore, folk say, and folk singing. That's me. I'll endure all of their "techniques" and "art forms" and "presentations" and "arrangements" and try to not throw nothing at nobody, but I be dam if I'm gonna hold back any good old truck driver's cuss words when they ask me to say what I think of Carl Sandburg's latest album, in spite of the good work he's done in the past. Because old Carl has been somewhere doing something that's made him sound like a monosexual dulcimer player having a cross between an opium dream and a wet nightmare. It hurts me to play these records of his. It would hurt the whole labor movement to mistake this for anything virile living or American — not always the words or the content, but goddam that kind of singing that sounds like two men sleeping together too long.

Lee tells me that I'm subconsciously setting up a big rock wall between myself and other and slicker projec-

Woody (far left) with the famous Almanac Singers (left to right): Millard Lampell, Bess Hawes Lomax, Pete Seeger, Arthur Stern, and Sis Cunningham, around 1943. Courtesy Marjorie Guthrie. ▶

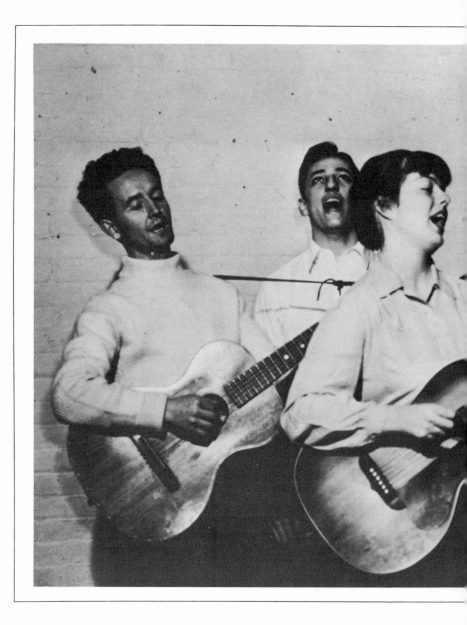

tionists, but maybe so, but then again on the other hand, of course you got five fingers, but on every finger you can count nine rock walls that these guys ain't only built between their selves and what is commonly called the American People, but they also go around with a spare rock wall in every pocket, and a whole slew of gravel highways running the wrong direction for change. The goddam radio, Hollywood, Tin Pan Alley, Broadway composers, they're the ones not to pattern after or pay attention to — but the only way to ever beat down that rock wall is by staying down on the old mamma ground with the miners, truck drivers, steel workers, cotton pickers, and five and ten cent store girls — and the waterfront strikes, and the women on the kitchen wagons, and the gals that wash out the piss chambers and gather up sticky towels in these here big hotels. I want to raise old billie hell when I hear a perfectly good looking, young, progressive theatre group even mention that word "shortage" of material. Because when you say you are short of material for the stage or anything else, you automatically say that you've forgotten all about the forty-eight states and their population, and that all current events on the other side of the ocean have slipped your mind, material, material — we ain't got no material, that's what they tell you everywhere you go. Hell's bells, ain't every day that you live material? Very few American cuss words can give me the feeling of relief necessary to rid me of 857565758 pounds of nervous tension, but when they say anything about a shortage of American Fighting Material, the only word that makes it possible for me to survive and remain alive is just pure old "bull shit."

We're bearing in mind a lot of things, and I think we ought to get together when we come to Lost Angels, but you will see a lot of good in the way the Almanacs do things, work, think, argue, raise hell, fight, run, fart, fall, and also march right through the walls of union halls, and win the friendship and many letters of reference and recommendation from the Union Heads — a work and a thing that is the first of its kind to ever come into the....

The letter stops in midsentence and I haven't found the rest. But you can get the idea from this how Woody's mind rambled and how, particularly when he was with the Almanacs, he was flying high, creating and spouting all over the place.

Huntington's Chorea
Means there's no help known
In the science of medicine
For me
And all of you Choreanites like me.

Because of my good medicine men
And all my good attendants
All look at me and say
By your words or by your whispers
There's just not no hope
Nor not no treatments known
To cure me of my dizzy [illegible]
Called chorea.

Maybe Jesus can think
Up a cure of some kind.©

Woody Guthrie, November 1954
Brooklyn State Hospital
Born to Win, p. 248

Afterword

AT THE OUTSET of this potpourri of memories, I wrote that Woody wouldn't let me alone. I have told this story to so many people who've been inspired by his life and work—to students and researchers and folksingers. Now I've written it all down, once and for all. I thought doing all this would exorcise Woody's ghost from my own spirit. But it hasn't. It has had the opposite effect.

Woody is still with me, now more than ever. He was twenty-six years old when we met and I was thirty-three. He'd be sixty-seven now, if he'd lived. I'm seventy-three, and still involved with Woody—writing about him and performing his songs with a group of other folks who wander from place to place making music and speaking the lines from his books and talking about the social and political events and atmosphere of the times in which he lived.

What is there so unique about this poet? Why is it that audiences are, for the most part, young people, not just older folks who might be reliving the past or basking in nostalgia? It's because Woody's songs and writings speak to today's problems and issues with passion and humor, as clearly as they did to what was happening in the thirties and forties. And also because his songs express a powerful love of this land and its people and a prophecy of "A better world a'comming."

Woody was a folk poet. You hear in his songs and stories the voices of his people, the sorrow and laughter, the strife, the joblessness and hunger, the great need for a better life. You hear the accents and dialects, the very voices of those Okies, Arkies, or Texans among whom he lived and grew, their struggle, suffering, and gut laughter. He was a folk poet because the voices of these people coursed through him like a transfusion of hot blood. That's why Woody thought that everybody could write songs and play music. He wanted everyone to sing about what was in their minds and hearts.

It's impossible to calculate the profound effect Woody Guthrie has had on other singers and writers, from Bob Dylan to the Beatles. Generations of Americans have been deeply influenced by the way he led his life and the way he expressed the most important things — personal feelings, politics, and social passions — all through his songs and writings.

Woody forged a weapon with his art. He knew it. He wrote across his guitar, "This Gittar Kills Fascists." But that guitar not only fought fascism and war, it was a sword in the struggle for decent wages and living conditions. Woody traveled the land seeking to organize, to get people together to fight for a better world, to wipe out discrimination against minorities and recognize the common enemy, the tyranny of a system that made a few rich and the many poor.

When I was a boy growing up in Chicago, you rarely saw people with guitars. Kids like me were pushed to take "music lessons" on the piano or violin. I remember sitting at the piano playing scales while my eyes were glued to the window watching my friends playing soft ball in the streets. Now, wherever you go, young people are playing guitars, mandolins, harmonicas, and a dozen other instruments. They play in their homes, in halls, and in the streets. Music is everywhere and thousands of people gather to listen to the songs. This is a great new thing, and Woody had a large part in making this happen.

Woody said that everyone can write songs and make music. May it be true that the day will come when all of us will indeed write our own songs and the voices of people from every land will mingle in a universal harmony. Perhaps, too, this mingling of voices will help to wipe out war and hunger.

If illness had not cut him down, we'd have had a much larger body of Woody's work, a whole treasury of new writings from his creative mind. I mourn this loss and the loss of his strong and hopeful spirit. And yet his spirit has affected me forever, because even with the bleak and clouded outlook for humanity today, I cannot help feel that the future will be bright. Even at seventy-three, I have a whole new life of writing, publishing, and performing. I think my old Woody would be pleased.

Sculpture by Natalie Leventhal. Photo by Emilio Rodriguez. ▶

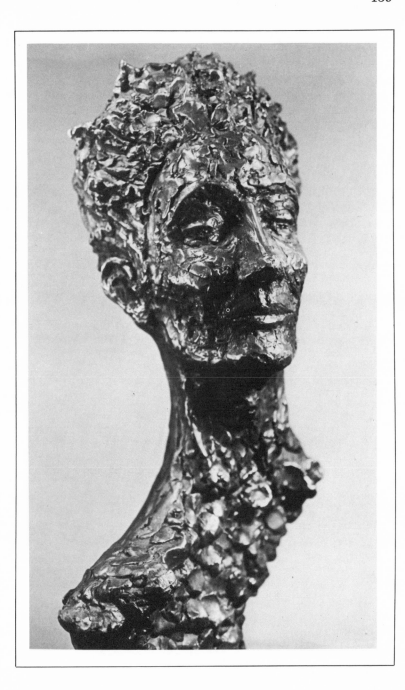

Bibliography

Davison, G. C., and J. M. Neale. *Abnormal Psychology*. New York: John Wiley, 1974.

Guthrie, Woody. *Born to Win*. New York: Macmillan, 1967.

———. *Bound for Glory*. New York: E. P. Dutton, 1943, 1967.

———. *Seeds of Man*. New York: E. P. Dutton, 1976.

———. *Woody Guthrie Folk Songs*. New York: Ludlow Music, 1963.

———. *Woody Sez*. New York: Grosset and Dunlap, 1975.

Leventhal, Harold, and Guthrie, Marjorie. *The Woody Guthrie Songbook*. New York: Grosset and Dunlap, 1976.

Robbin, Edward. "David Carradine as Woody Guthrie." *City*, September 23, 1975, pp. 26-28.

Yurchenco, Henrietta. *A Might Hard Road: The Life of Woody Guthrie*. New York: McGraw-Hill, 1970.